QUANTUM ~~RETIREMENT:~~
WALTZING IN COSMIC BABYLON

To Ed and Joan
Sturgeon — with
all good wishes.

How to tell if YOU are descended from a space alien

WEEKLY WORLD

NEWS

November 1, 1988   30587   65¢

Hooters Beauty Makes River Run Backwards!

Terminal patients were weighed before and after they died!

HUMAN SOUL WEIGHS ⅓,000TH OF AN OUNCE

'This proves there IS life after death,' say top scientists

Painting of Elvis weeps real tears!

DAN MCDONALD & SUSAN LUCCI

New Revelations!

Gutsy girl swims herself to death!

DEVIL'S SKULL DISCOVERED — In Mobile, Alabama!

#186 - "LET'S HEAR IT FOR THE *NEWS*"

QUANTUM RETIREMENT:

Waltzing in Cosmic Babylon

201 Essays by Dan McDonald

Illustrations by Fred Maes

THE GULF COAST HUMANITIES CONSORTIUM
Mobile, Alabama

ISBN 0-9659311-0-2

Published by The Gulf Coast Humanities Consortium, 2001 Old Bay Front Drive, Mobile, AL 36615

Printed and bound in the United States of America

Quantum Retirement is a registered trademark of Daniel McDonald

INTRODUCTION

I've been writing these essays since June 1993, when I retired from the English Department of the University of South Alabama. My pieces run from half-a-page to two-pages long. My genre is the short-short essay.

The subjects reflect my several roles. I am a happy husband, a proud father, a convivial male, a teacher, a writer, and a senior-citizen. (Today I am 69, going on 30.) I am a logician who writes books on argument, so I enjoy tabloid stories ("BIGFOOT TALKS!"). I am a Roman Catholic who wrote a book on the Bible. (A loyal son of the Church, I make it a rule never to drink beer until it's noon, in Vatican City.) I've lost a lot of eyesight in recent years, but I'm living with that.

Most of my writing is intended as humor. But it's not standup-comic funny. It's really funny. *All my stories are true.*

How funny am I? Well, a few years ago, Irene and I each had an article in the *National Catholic Reporter*. Mine was a witty piece about Catholic marriage. Hers was a review of Edward Erikson's *Solzhenitsyn: The Moral Vision*. Months later at a party in Atlanta, I met a HarperCollins editor who said she had read both pieces. "Yours," she remembered, "was funnier."

A man who's funnier than Solzhenitsyn's moral vision should get out a book.

ACKNOWLEDGEMENTS

With a book of memoirs, I'm tempted to acknowledge everyone I've ever known. I'll spare you that.

I want to thank Fred Maes for his friendship and his wonderful illustrations.

I thank Jud Blakely and Larry Burton for their comradeship and good values.

My wife proofread this book and found herself on half the pages. I thank her for her tolerance and good-will. Irene has made retirement a joy.

DMc

TABLE OF CONTENTS

#180 - "HIT IT BIG AT THE BELLE

(1) Cosmic Babylon

A good deal of thought and research went into titling this book.

I think these are witty, provocative essays. They say retirement is pleasant, our world is a crazy place, and lots of things are funny if you look at them. I'm confident people will enjoy the book. But no publisher will print it and fewer readers will look at it if it doesn't have a jazzy title. So last week, I went to Barnes & Noble to identify the words that commonly appear in best-selling titles. I came home with a list.

The words which challenge the American mind are *cosmic, unleashing, mutant, midnight, cellulite, dancing, Armageddon, Madison County, syndrome, virgin, quantum, Power!, Nostradamus, passion, myth, Elvis, crisis, Babylon,* and *conspiracy.* So, dismissing every moral principle I ever had (both of them), I came up with a commercial title. My book is now called *Quantum Retirement: Waltzing in Cosmic Babylon.*

I hope this helps.

(2) The Last Blue Jeans

It's hard to give up old ways, and I'm not sure I'm ready to.

Last month, I went to Gayfers to buy a new pair of jeans. (My old pair is a dozen years old.) I told the clerk — a serious 20-year-old girl — I wanted some jeans. She asked if I wanted Guess or Calvin Klein or Jordache or Bugle Boy or ... I said I wanted regular jeans. When she mentioned Levi's, I said, "Yeah, that's what I'll have." She asked if I wanted 560 or 550 or 545 or Silver Medal or ... I repeated I wanted plain jeans, the kind I've worn since 1950. Undaunted, she offered me flare leg, straight leg, button fly, stretch fabric, loose fit, relaxed fit, boot cut... It took ten minutes to establish that, by my standards, Levi's 501 is the traditional brand. She asked if I wanted them stone-washed, and I said regular jeans would be all right. Finally, as she carried my pair to the sales-counter, she apologized. "I'm sorry," she said. "We only have these in blue."

Well, that experience is over now, and I won't have to do it again. At my age, the new jeans should last me the rest of my life.

(3) An Invasion of Privacy

On WMOB this morning, the preacher on *The Voice of Truth* said, "Now let us pray together, each for our own peculiar needs." This bothers me.

Who told him about my peculiar needs?

(4) The Celestial Banquet

At Mass yesterday, the theme was humility. In Luke's gospel, Jesus told his followers not to take the first place when they sit down at a meal. They might be asked to move. They should take the last place so the host can say, "Friend, come up higher." I worry about this counsel.

What if the host doesn't say "Friend, come up higher"?

Isn't there a lot of pride in taking that last seat? What's so special about phony humility? I know my relative importance. Can't I take a middle place? Or can't I fudge it and take a seat one or two places above where I belong? No one will make a fuss about that.

In his sermon, Father Wall spoke of the heavenly banquet where we will all sit in our true place and Jesus himself will serve us. This is a lovely metaphor, but I worry about Jesus serving a hundred billion souls. Won't it take a while to get our meal? I hope someone is passing out before-dinner drinks.

And immediately I speculated: What will we eat at the celestial banquet? (Since we're all dead, we can dispense with the health menu.) If this is ideal perfection, I know what we'll eat. We'll have meat-loaf sandwiches, potato salad, and Heineken beer. Of course, with that as the meal, I'll hate waiting around to be served.

Come to think of it, I may grab that seat up front.

(5) "I'll Show That Bitch"

I just heard an interview at the Westminster Dog Show where an owner announced his plans for his award-winning Pomeranian. He said. "I'll show that bitch all next summer: then I'll retire her." It was gratifying to hear someone say. "I'll show that bitch" in a loving and tender voice. I'd never heard that before.

(6) Questions You Can't Answer

Irene and I are just back from a three-week Elderhostel in Spain, and friends ask how it was. We can't tell them.

What can you say about a week at the Prado? We had four lectures (with slides) telling us about El Greco, Zurbaran, Velasquez, Murillo, and Ribera. Then we had afternoons at the Prado seeing the paintings. We visited the Goya Chapel and the Picasso Museum.

We saw incredible Christian sculpture at the Episcopal Museum in Vic. We visited ancient churches and cloisters around Barcelona. It was overwhelming. The trip gave us new insights into religion, art, war, nature, and ourselves – and already you're bored hearing about it.

There are things you can't talk about. They are usually moments of sudden insight or intense feeling. What can you say when someone asks:

- How's little Rebecca? She's nearly a year old, isn't she?
- Did you get anything out of your retreat at the Visitation Convent?
- So this is Boswell. Is he a nice dog?
- Did you and Mandy have a fun weekend in Atlanta?
- That's supposed to be a fine production *Don Giovanni*. Did you enjoy it?

When the question calls for superlatives, you might as well forget it. There are no words. Say, "Oh, it (he, she, they) was very nice. How have you been?"

With a dear friend, late at night, maybe when the alcohol flows, you can try giving an honest answer.

(7) The Real Me Is Somebody Special

Next month I'm flying to Wisconsin to attend a reunion of the Black River Falls High School, Class of '45. I'm preparing for it in the traditional way. I'm losing 10 pounds. I'm buying a new wardrobe (mainly blue items which my color-analyst recommends). I'm getting a neat haircut, and I plan to have a professional manicure and a professional shoeshine just before I leave Mobile. I'm using Rembrandt toothpaste to make my smile sparkle, and I may visit a tanning-salon. I'll look great at the reunion, but I'm having identity problems.

As I was making these preparations, I ran across a Clairol ad which told women "Maybe the Real You Is a Blonde." Hey, I know I shouldn't be blond, but the line makes me wonder about things. Is it possible the real me is slim, bronzed, well-coiffed and manicured, beautifully tailored, and exquisitely elegant? If so, where has he been since 1957? Has he been hiding out someplace?

I imagine the real me traveling the world in style. He sails the QE2 (first class, of course) to spend the opera season in Vienna. In white dinner-jacket and black tie, he dines regularly at Maxim's and has serious conversations with the wine-steward. (His French is impeccable.) Part of the New York social scene, he lives at Trump Tower, dives a BMW, and wears Georgio Armani suits. He attended the opening night of *Sunset Boulevard* with a model named Francesca.

Is that what the real me has been doing all these years? God, I wish I'd been there.

(8) A Religious Test

Here's how to identify an Irish Catholic. Say the name "Jimmy Swaggart." Where some people might get emotional and bluster about hypocrisy and the horrors of fleshly lust, the Irishman will shrug and say, "Sorry about him." If you push the issue, he may add, "Those things happen." If you push it further, he'll say, "Hey, forget it. Can I get you a beer?"

I have a name for this attitude. I call it "Christianity."

#2 - "THE LAST BLUE JEANS"

(9) Non-Verbal Communication

At a General Semantics conference in San Diego some years ago, I attended a program on non-verbal communication. It demonstrated how much we can tell bout people just by looking at them. The man in charge made us divide in pairs, each of us paired with someone we didn't know. Then we had to fill out a questionnaire describing our partner.

I was paired with a handsome lady in her mid-thirties. (I enjoyed studying her.) In about five minutes, I stood up and told the group she was a drama teacher, a runner, a mother of three children (two boys and a girl), and the wife of a doctor. The woman gasped in amazement. I was exactly right.

Actually it wasn't that hard. Many of us were English teachers, and she looked pizzazzy (with a sporty, short haircut). To me, that said drama. Her slim build told me she was a runner. Her wedding-ring said she was married, and it was easy to assume children. Women of her generation tended to have three. "Two boys and a girl" was just a guess, but a reasonable one. The lady was wearing a handsome sports-outfit, with salmon-color pants and a beige sweater. Very tasteful. On the collar of the sweater was a design of the same salmon-color. This meant it was an ensemble. And it was perfect; so it was expensive. That meant money, and money (for me) meant doctor. I was right all down the line, and everyone applauded.

Then the lady got up and analyzed me. She said, among other things, that I was a California stockbroker, a bachelor who owned a house on the beach and drove a Corvette. The program broke up before I had a chance to correct her. I'm not sure I would have anyway.

(10) Arguments Against Daylight-Saving Time

In last week's *Mobile Register*, a woman said she didn't like daylight-saving time. It just gave the sun an extra hour to burn up her grass. That's the second best argument I've heard on this issue.

The best appeared 30 years ago in the *Wisconsin State Journal*. (I just found it in my clippings-file.) A man named Bennett insisted that changing the time was unnatural. It violated the divine plan. After all, he argued, God made the sun. God made the earth. God drew the meridian lines on the earth. God...

You know Mr. Bennett was serving an all-powerful god. Who else could paint that equator line so straight?

(11) Tabloid Geography

When friends ask why I read the *National Enquirer*, the *Sun*, and the *Weekly World News*, I say, "Only because I subscribe." But there's more to it than that. Tabloid readers live in a bigger world.

Think about it. In recent months, I've seen the face on Mars, and I've discovered Mexico's Santiago Valley (which is a secret UFO base). I've had continuing revelations about the Bermuda Triangle (where tourists saw the ghost of Al Capone), Atlantis (which has now been located, on the moon), and Loch Ness (where Nessie, the monster, recently had a 2000-pound baby).

I'm relearning the geography of the United States. I can now distinguish Lake Erie (home of the mysterious Black Monster) from Lake Superior (home of

the prehistoric 80-foot shark). I study the map of
California and Oregon as Bigfoot stomps into new places.
My scripture reading is more immediate since I've seen
the Colorado site where archeologists discovered the
bones of Adam and Eve — and the Pennsylvania hill
where they found Noah's Ark. And, of course, I'm
tracing Elvis sightings — from Hawaii to Blacksburg,
Virginia, to upstate New York, to Kalamazoo, Michigan.
(Recent activity has focused around St. Louis.)

The tabloids are teaching me a lot. I just
researched the Valley of the Pharaohs in an article
titled "Great Pyramids Are Upside Down!" The *Weekly
World News* says they were supposed to have flat tops
so alien spacecraft could land there. Who else will tell
me this?

(12) Self-Referencing Sentences

Yes, Virginia, there *are* self-referencing sentences. These
are lines which comment on themselves. Famous
examples include "This sentence is false" and "This
sentence no verb." For Christmas this year, I'm giving
my two best friends rectangular marble paperweights.
Each carries a black plastic top with the inscription: IF
YOU HAD FINISHED READING THIS SENTENCE,

(13) Blame It on Dr. Jekyll

Oh, Lord, they're suing the tobacco companies again.

Nobody is responsible for anything any more. If
you smoke for 50 years and get lung-cancer, you can
sue Philip Morris. If you drink half-a-dozen martinis
and crash your Cutlass into an oak-tree, you can sue
the city-engineers, or the lounge which served you that
last drink, or (more likely) General Motors. If your life
is a mess, you can find a psychiatrist who'll assure you

it's your mother's fault. If you're 150 pounds overweight, blame it on your genes. The popular theme is "I didn't do it, Officer. I was out of town when it happened."

And this can be true. Things do happen to people which aren't their fault. *But not everything*.

I remember a rich line from the TV production of *Dr. Jekyll and Mr. Hyde*. (It starred Jack Palance.) Jekyll, you remember, discovers a potion which turns him into Edward Hyde, a creature who roams London doing monstrous things. When Jekyll decides not to drink the potion any more, the change occurs spontaneously, and Hyde continues his evil deeds. At the climax, Utterson is holding a gun threatening to shoot Hyde, who cunningly says, "Remember if you shoot me, you'll shoot Henry Jekyll." Utterson's response is central. He says, "*Hyde, this has nothing to do with you*. Dr. Jekyll is responsible. He knows he is."

That's a heavy truth. But I'm not sure who knows it any more.

(14) Ad Apologies

Have you noticed that some TV ads sound like confessions?

I think "Rolling Rock — Same as it ever was" and "Old Milwaukee — It doesn't get any better than this" sound more like apologies than promises. And how about the Camero line: "What can you expect from a country that invented rock and roll?" Somehow I'm not encouraged.

And now there's the TV ad for *Silk Stalkings*. It says, "See it on USA — and nowhere else." That could be a boast, I suppose. To me, it sounds like doctors have just localized the tumor.

(15) <u>The Voice of Old Age</u>

Last week my friend Audrey asked me to speak to her Social Gerontology class at South Alabama. I was to take 25 minutes discussing the biological, psychological, social, and social-psychological aspects of aging. What they wanted was someone to stand up and say, "This is what it's like to be old." I said I'd be happy to do it.

Before the class, Audrey took me aside and asked, with much delicacy, if I would try to stay up-beat. Apparently, she feared a depressing talk about arthritis, prostate problems, the boredom of retirement, separation from family, the death of friends, etc. I asked her, "When have you ever known me not to be upbeat?"

So Monday night, I faced a class of sociology students, most of them in their 20s. I began with a brief survey of recent activity. I said, "I'm pleased to be here tonight. Last month, my wife and I spent two weeks in London. Right after that, we spent two weeks down at the Gulf. Last week, we stayed with my daughter in St. Croix, where I did some scuba-diving. We're happy to be back in town." I let that hang in the air for 10 seconds. Then I smiled and said, "It's hell being old."

Right there, I taught them a lot about the biological, psychological, social, and social-psychological aspects of aging.

(16) <u>Drug-Free in Wisconsin</u>

At my 50th high-school reunion, classmate Bruce Behlow spelled out the difference between teenagers of our generation and teenagers today. There were three

reasons why we didn't get involved with drugs. "First,"
he said, "we were raised with traditional family values.
Second, we had common-sense. We knew that events
had consequences."

Then Bruce just sat there; he was silent. "What's
the third reason?" I asked. "Don't you remember, Dan?"
he laughed, "we didn't have drugs back then."

(17) Hooters and Good Values

The last time Jud, Larry and I were at Gulf Shores, we
ate lunch at Hooters and had our usual great
time. When we left, however, I began to wonder about
Hooters values.

Everything at the restaurant was tasty. The
cheeseburgers were huge; the french-fries were plentiful
and heavily salted. We drank several rounds of Corona
beer. The waitresses were charming, full-figured girls.
They ranged in age from 21 to 21-and-a-half. They
wore orange short-shorts and cut-off T-shirts. All
waistlines were trim and visible. The girls were
friendly; they laughed a lot. They identified themselves
as Bambi and Judi and Candi — and they didn't have
last names. After a joyous hour, we walked out, and
Larry asked a rhetorical question. He said, "Man, is
that what you want out of life?"

Breathing the cool air of the parking-lot, I found
myself saying "No."

At 67, a man should have better values. I
assured my friends I really prefer fruit and vegetables
to that greasy food. (A careful diet will keep me
rolling through my 70s.) I said it's healthier if men
drink beer in moderation. I reminded them that
women are full human-beings, and they shouldn't be
seen just as sex-objects. I said all this, and I felt

proud of my mature values. As we approached our car, I walked a little taller.

And my nose grew an inch-and-a-half.

(18) The On-the-Make Crowd

Last night my writer-friend Jud complained about language that frustrates him. Opening the *Mobile Press*, he showed me a reference to an "on-the-make crowd." He said, "Look at that. They have a 2-letter word, followed by a 3-letter word, followed by a 4-letter word, followed by a 5-letter word." I asked what the problem was. "I hate that," he yelled. "I just hate that."

A man can sit at his word-processor too long.

(19) Wolfman Fantasies

"Even a man who is pure in heart
And says his prayers by night
May become a wolf when the wolf-bane
blooms
And the moon shines full and bright."

It's one thing to enjoy the old Lon Chaney movies. It's something else to hear your doctor say you might have wolfman disease. You get mixed feelings.

Because I have a reddish hardening on the back of my hands, I went to see Dr. Honkanen last week. She asked the usual questions about diet and skin-contact, then ordered blood and urine samples. Also, she felt the hair on my temples and looked for some growing between my eyebrows. She said my problem could be an allergy, or liver dysfunction, or a vitamin deficiency — or it might even be a form of porphyria. At worst, this causes skin discoloration, heavy hair-

#19 - "WOLFMAN FANTASIES"

growth, and violent psychotic episodes. It can be fatal. She assured me I probably have contact dermatitis. We'll know next week when the tests come back.

What's it like thinking you may be a werewolf? I have twin responses. I am distressed, of course, but not much. The chance I have the disease is remote. Mainly, I am *thrilled*! After all, I am a man. I was raised championing male values: strength, domination, virility, individualism, privacy, and freedom from civilized restraint. In Black River Falls, Wisconsin, Bob Huntley and I grew up with Wolfman movies and relished cinematic fantasies. We imagined being Larry Talbot, marked with the sign of the pentagram, and terrorizing the countryside. (We were especially concerned, as I remember, about terrorizing the Werner sisters.) Our motto was, "Give me a full moon, and I'll rule the world."

Now (hypothetically, anyway), I may have my fantasy. And it comes when I'm 68 and can use the macho reinforcement. If you meet me at Bel Air Mall, you'll see the difference. I'll walk taller; I'll swing my arms wider; I'll leer at the girls more openly. In McDonald's, I'll order my Quarter-pounder blood-rare, and I'll growl if it takes them awhile to fix it. I'll disdain the crowds around me. I'll tell myself, "I run this place."

So my hands itch a little, big deal! I'm feeling restless, vigorous, invincible. And these are my everyday emotions. Give me a full moon and . . .

(20) Easy Choices

Yesterday Carolyn Dunnam asked me if I'd like to spend a week at the Gulf in January teaching an Elderhostel class. I said sure. And she said, "Oh, Dan, you're always so nice." This is the way things work for me.

People are always offering me something wonderful, then giving me a choice about taking it. At the University of Wisconsin, Annabelle would phone and say, "Hi. I just finished my term-paper. You want to come over?" When I flew on my daughter's airline pass, the gate-agent usually said, "I can put you in First Class. Would you prefer that?" Irene routinely says, "I may make shrimp-gumbo for supper tonight. Is that OK?"

The ultimate "choice" occurred in June of 1960, when a Catholic Social Services lady took Irene and me to see a baby we were eligible to adopt. There, dressed in blue, lay 10-week-old Molly smiling up at us. We held her and talked about her for half an hour; then the lady said, "Go home now and decide if this is the child you want." (At this point, of course, I would kill for that baby.) "Fine," I said, "we'll go home and talk about it."

I was reminded of happy choices when Irene and I were in St. Croix last week. We stayed at the Chenay Bay resort. The outdoor bar served a delicious homemade dressing we could put on salads or seafood. There were two large bottles to choose from. One said "Italian." So did the other.

(21) Cinnamon Research

Neurologists at the Smell and Taste Treatment Research Foundation (Chicago) bring us the news. Trying to establish sexual motivation, they monitored penile blood-flow in 25 medical students as they sniffed a range of scents. Only cinnamon-rolls turned the men on. This is an important finding.

For generations, mothers have warned their daughters about evil men, men who are out only after one thing. Now we know what it is.

(22) Life in the Cloister

Some years ago, responding to a perceived exodus, a New York City publicist came up with a slogan. Recalling the City's vast energy and opportunity, he wrote, "When you leave New York, you ain't going anywhere." I always liked that line, but I was amazed when it came to me in a 13th century Spanish cloister.

A cloister, you remember, is a place where monks spent their lives in silent meditation. They did manual labor and attended Mass and group prayer, but they gave most of their time to contemplation. In quiet gardens, they faced the truth. They thought about themselves, their gifts and mortality, about other people and human events, about the nature of things. They stared into the mystery. They thought about God and their relationship with divinity. That's what they did.

I'm drawn to this life of quiet and honesty, but I don't think I could handle it. I'd enjoy meditation, but the hours would mount up and I'd get edgy. Soon, I'd try to smuggle in Boswell's *Life of Johnson* and a lap-top computer. I'd want Irene to visit me on weekends.

For other men, the monks who could live in a cloister, it must have been a rewarding life. They were complete in themselves. They didn't require things. God and reality were all they needed.

I thought about this on our trip to Spain last month when we visited the cloister in Terragona. It was deserted – almost. In the middle of the garden, lying in the sun, was a large, gray cat. For me, it was a perfect symbol. If there's any creature that is complete, that doesn't need things, that keeps its own counsel, it's a cat. I was envious. I want to be more like that.

If I were a better man, God and quiet and contemplation would be enough. The monastery would provide it all. I'd know, if I left the cloister, I wouldn't be going anywhere.

(23) Art Criticism in the 90s

As I write this, the current edition of the *Weekly World News* has an article explaining Mona Lisa's mysterious smile. It quotes a French dental expert, Dr. Andre Garcin, who insists da Vinci's beauty was a battered wife. She smiles that way because she has lost her front teeth.

I love this because it opens a new academic area: medical art-criticism. Now we can see the real problem of Picasso's angular men (arthritis) and Rubens' lush nudes (glandular dysfunction). Michelangelo's *Moses* is sitting very erect. Should we suspect hemorrhoids?

(24) Excitement City, U.S.A.

I cherish moments of minimalist pleasure. They aren't immediately thrilling, but they're fun to think about afterwards.

A few years ago, we lived across the street from the Humburgers. They were a nice couple, but their scottie, Sylvester, yapped all day and all night. Once at 2:00 a.m., Irene woke me. She said, "Listen, Dan. Sylvester's not barking." I listened and he wasn't.

In Wales last month, Irene bought a bottle of Numark Intensive Hand Creme. When she rubbed it on, she told me, "This is unusual. It's unscented." I said, "Really?" She said, "Yes, smell it." So I did.

I told her I hadn't had such a thrill since the day her brother-in-law entertained me in Washington, D.C. Joe wasn't sure what an English professor would like, so he drove 20 miles out in the country to show me the house where Joyce Kilmer's brother used to live.

Make no mistake, I enjoyed these moments. Let Mick Jagger live in the fast lane.

(25) Obedience Is a State of Mind

I wonder that my neighbors, the Melichars, are paying $170 to have a professional train their Dalmatian. I don't need to send my pets to obedience-school. I have a golden retriever (Boswell) and a white tomcat (Hodge), and around my house we have perfect obedience. When Boswell barks at the back-door or Hodge meows at the patio window, immediately I leap up and let them in.

(26) Just Like 1944

I was a facilitator at the Elderhostel classes held at Brookley last week. (I've also been a teacher and a participant in these programs.) And I had a moment of revelation.

On Friday, the Ballroom Dance class taught jitterbugging, and I watched a dozen couples (all in their 60s and beyond) bouncing to a Glenn Miller beat. The music and the dance-style flashed me back to Black River Falls, Wisconsin, in the 1940s. "Golly," I thought, "they look like the girls who drove me nuts in high-school." And, of course, the revelation followed: "Those *are* the girls who drove me nuts in high-school."

Was I disturbed seeing my teenage beauties 50 years later? No way! Sure, they were older now. Their weight had shifted. They had graying hair and some wrinkles. But these women were full of life. They weren't sitting home cleaning bureau-drawers and worrying about their grandchildren. They'd come from all over the country to see Mobile and make new friends, to learn about Dixieland Jazz, Historic Homes, and Ballroom Dance. I saw them smiling; their eyes were bright. They stepped around the dance-floor swinging to "In the Mood." "Damn," I thought, "they *still* look good!"

I hope my Black River Falls girls have aged as well. I suspect they have.

(27) In Defense of Men

My daughter Rebecca was having social problems a while ago, and she called me up to announce, "All men are pigs!" What does a father say to that?

I told her the problem cuts two ways. I mentioned that the gentleman's club I belong to – the Gulf Coast Humanities Consortium – has two main topics of discussion: 1) "What do women want?" And 2) "How about another beer?" Rebecca asked if that's all we talked about. I told her, "Sometimes we leave out the part about the women."

(28) What Does a Rat Know?

It was a rich moment. Last Friday morning, Dr. Steve Itaya of South Alabama's medical faculty, lectured Odyssey (a local Elderhostel group) on the workings of the human brain. He mentioned tests done on rats and monkeys and studies of human abnormality. Illustrating the brain's incredible specialization, he spoke of a small section which governs face-recognition. If there is an occlusion in this area, a man will be unable to recognize his wife. He may identify her by her clothes, speech, and manner, but he won't know her by looking at her face. At this point, a lady raised her hand and asked a question. She said, "Can you reproduce this condition in rats?"

This was followed by a significant pause. Dr. Itaya looked up and stared at us. He surveyed the audience. The pause seemed to say "Who are these people?" and "What can you expect from Caucasians?" Finally, he gave a low-key response expressed with oriental impassivity. He said, "It would be challenging to design a test which will measure that variable." I guess he told us.

Can rats recognize faces? I think work on this issue will have to be done by mentalists. I remember the gifted psychic celebrated in a Woody Allen essay. The man could, with 100 percent accuracy, guess any number being thought of by a squirrel.

(29) A Triumph over Jargon

In my technical-writing seminars, I tell students to avoid unnatural-sounding jargon. I give them the line "Please advise availability of key personnel" and award a prize to the person who can best translate that into English.

Bright students usually come up with "Who is available?" and "What people can you send me?" The all-time winner came from Michael Roberts, an International Paper engineer. He offered, "Where is Leroy?"

(30) Theology at the Pink Pony Pub

Now for a theological insight.

#30 - "THEOLOGY AT THE PINK PONY PUB"

Some years ago, after I had taught Old Testament all week, Mike Hanna and I and some friends drove down to Gulf Shores to drink beer. We based ourselves on the porch of the Pink Pony Pub. After a couple of hours of laughter and Rolling Rock, Mike and the others went down to the beach. (The porch at the Pony has steps leading down to the sand, and halfway down is a landing with rails on both sides.) They called me to join them. Full of beer and enthusiasm, I skipped down to the landing. Then I thought, "I could vault over the side here. It's only eight feet up. I've done that before." So I vaulted over. When I was in the air, it came to me "Yes, I've done this before, but it was 40 years ago." I landed hard, of course, and ripped several muscles in my side.

When I walked into my Old Testament class on Monday, my side still ached. Then we began the Book of Job. I had to explain why God lets bad things happen to good people. As sharp pains ran down my side, it occurred to me God wasn't responsible for everything.

(31) Daddy and Rex

One night 20 years ago, the kids and I were sitting in the family-room with our beloved Rex (a german-shepherd / golden-retriever combination). At one point, out of nowhere, Molly said, "Did you notice? Daddy and Rex look alike." How should I respond to that?

My reaction is straight-forward. I've told the children over the years that, when I die, my money will be divided equally among them. But Molly gets the house.

(32) Boredom in Ecclesiastes

I love the Book of Ecclesiastes, but not the first part.
There, you remember, the Preacher is unhappy. He
complains that the same things happen over and over.
He's bored:

> All rivers run into the sea;
> Yet the sea is not full:
> Unto the place from whence the rivers come,
> Thither they return again.
> All things are full of labor,
> Man cannot utter it.
> The eye is not satisfied with seeing,
> Nor the ear filled with hearing.
> The thing that hath been,
> It is that which shall be;
> And that which is done is that which shall
>   be done,
> And there is no new thing under the sun.

That's memorable poetry, but I don't buy it. I think
the Preacher was having a bad day.

I'm 66, and I've seen a lot. But I don't get bored
with the same old things. Should I complain, "Oh God,
here's another sunrise, and some fresh coffee, and a
cheese-omelet. Take them away, Lord. I've seen
enough babies and pretty women and golden retrievers.
I walked the Irish countryside last summer; don't send
me back. And now Irene wants to spend a weekend at
the Gulf. No way! It will just be Heineken beer and
crab-salad and jazz music and making love and walking
on the beach. I've done all that. I'm bored. Show
me something different, Lord. Show me something
new."

See how weird that attitude is? I can make
sense of the Ecclesiastes lines, but I have to imagine

the Preacher is suffering clinical depression.

I think of all this because I just heard Kurt Masur and the New York Philharmonic perform Beethoven's Fifth on PBS. If there ever was a musical "war-horse" that has been played and played, it's the Fifth. But the program wasn't dull. It was powerful, challenging, life-affirming. Had I been there, I'd have been the man with goose-pimples on both arms, applauding wildly, and shouting "One more time!"

(33) Of Bourbon and Cigarettes

Today I'm a healthy 67-year-old, and I want to go on record that I have *not* given up whiskey or cigarettes. It's just that I haven't used them for ten years.

I was reminded of this last month when we flew to St. Croix to visited Molly and Ed and his 15-year-old labrador, Midnight. The dog is pretty much blind; he stumbles into things; he sometimes messes the floor. But he is much loved. After supper one night, Molly started feeding him some greasy chicken-scraps, and Irene warned they were bad for his health. Then we looked at Midnight and laughed. What can hurt him now?

I fanaticize about a day (years from now) when Irene and I are leaving Dr. Broughton's office, and he's told us the cancer has now spread into my liver. As we get in the car, I'll say, "Honey, let's swing around to the tobacco shop. Then we can go by the liquor-store. Maybe there's a sale on Wild Turkey."

(34) The Road to Grace

At a recent Elderhostel meeting, a lady praised me for my good attitude. She said, "I'm impressed at how well you handle your blindness." (Actually, I'm only half blind.) She said, "You're so gracious about it."

She is right. I am taking the situation well. I don't complain. I tell jokes when I stumble into things. I am calm when I spill beer on strangers. I stay upbeat.

This attitude toward blindness is one I came to slowly. First, I said "Shit!" a lot. Then I assigned blame. God should have given this handicap to someone who deserves it more. (I was willing to provide a list of names.) Doctor Blazdon should have identified my glaucoma sooner. And, of course, Irene was culpable in many ways. Some nights, when she led me into the house, she didn't immediately turn on every light we own. Sometimes she'd put a glass of water on the dinner-table. (It's transparent, and I knock it over.) She even commented when I trailed coffee down the hall or spilled thousand-island dressing on our tablecloth.

I complained. I fussed about the indifference and inefficiency around me. Ace TV didn't fix the set right; it still has a fuzzy picture. The Shell station never cleaned our windshield enough. Stores at Springdale Mall were poorly lit. University buildings always had a step up (or a step down) that appeared unexpectedly. The men's room at Ruby Tuesday was in a dark, inaccessible corner. Burger King always filled my coffee cup too full, then hid their cream and sugar where nobody can find them. Apple should have put a larger cursor on my Macintosh. The hymnals at St. Ignatius Church had tiny, unreadable print. It was a conspiracy! I complained about bartenders and elevators and stairwells and . . .

I could only grouse so long. Then I had to admit I had a problem, and it was nobody's fault. So now I live with bad eyesight and stumble around amiably.

But I can't take credit for having a good attitude. I tried everything else first.

After a while, all that's left is grace.

(35) Stock Market Euphemisms

I love the language of the stock-market. Prices don't just "rise." They "enjoy a rally," or they "surge upward." And prices never "fall." The market undergoes a "consolidation" or a "correction." (To quote my broker-son, Nicholas: "A correction is when you lose your ass.")

I heard an interview on CNBC the other night. Panel-members kept asking the analyst, "What should one do if there is a market correction?" Later they asked, "What if it is a major correction?" Finally, someone asked, "What about a really major correction?"

That's heavy language. I think of an 8.1 earthquake as a major correction. The Second Coming of Christ will be a really major correction.

(36) Fair Is Fair

Sometimes a father has to speak up. Several months ago, Irene and I were in St. Croix to see our daughter Molly marry Ed Buckley. The day after the wedding, we sat with his parents discussing the event. (The Buckleys, incidentally, are just like us: she is real smart, and he drinks too much.) We were talking about how nice the sailboat ceremony was. Ruth said she hadn't lost a son; she had gained a daughter. Irene echoed that she had gained a son. Chuck Buckley said, "Yeah, Dan, we just made a trade." I whispered to him, "Nothing personal, Chuck, but you need to throw in a Cadillac Coupe de Ville."

(37) The Magnetic Field

As I write this, I am wearing a handsome bracelet.
It's bronze and has a stretch watchband construction.
I mailed off $16 for it. It is a Stress Bracelet.

Around it are nine magnets. They provide 800
gauss of energy and keep my body in a magnetic field.
They will align my ions. This isn't AMA medicine, I
know that. But the ad assured me, "In Asia, the
benefits of providing magnetic fields are well known
and widely practiced."

Is the bracelet helping me? The issue came up
at an ABC conference in Phoenix, where I spoke on
talismans and the language used to sell them. During
the presentation, I wore my blue suit; around my neck
was Madame Zarina's talisman, and on my wrist the
Stress Bracelet. Among the questions following my
speech, a woman asked if the magic artifacts were
doing me any good. I said, "Hey, who's up front giving
this talk? Who's out of town traveling on university
money? Without my necklace and bracelet, I could be
home mowing the lawn."

(38) Sex in Oklahoma

Recently an Oklahoma legislator, Cleta Deather,
introduced a bill which would make it illegal for a man
to have sex with a woman 1) if he didn't first warn
her of the physical and emotional dangers involved, and
2) if he didn't get her permission *in writing*. I see
passion waning as she asks, "Explain to me again about
the HIV virus." I see frustration rising as he says,
"Dammit, Sylvia, if you kept the pencil in the desk-
drawer, you wouldn't lose it all the time." Fortunately
for everybody, the bill didn't pass.

(39) St. Paul and My Cat

Hodge is a large, white tomcat we've had for two years. He's comfortable to be around, but it took a while to tame him. I learned from the experience. I learned what St. Paul was trying to tell the Galatians.

We got the cat from the Grahams, a family that lived four blocks away. Hodge had been a church-cat before they took him. When they found he fought with their other cats, they brought him to us. We put him on our screened-in back-porch and kept him there. We put out Cat Chow and water, and there was a litter-box across the room. Every day Irene and I went out to pet him and say nice things. Hodge ignored us. He just lay in his corner and looked up toward his old house.

After two weeks, I thought I could take him outside. On a bright Saturday afternoon, I carried a dish of liver catfood and some ribbon we could play with. Then I opened the door thinking Hodge would join me on the grass. *Whoosh!* He was gone. He just disappeared. That night Mrs. Graham phoned to say the cat had returned to them. The next morning, her husband brought Hodge back, and we put him out on the porch again.

The following week, we tried everything: tuna catfood, regular petting, loving words. No response. Hodge wouldn't even look at us. Finally I said things couldn't go on like that, and I let the cat out. Of course, he disappeared. But I did call the Grahams and ask them not to feed him or take him in.

Three days passed. Then one afternoon, I was reading on the porch when I saw a white cat coming across the grass. Hodge walked very slowly, but finally he came to our screen-door. I didn't say anything; I

#32 - "BOREDOM IN ECCLESIASTES"

just opened the door and stepped back. About a minute passed. Then Hodge walked through the door. From that moment, he was our cat.

What's the point of all this? Well, I'd written a book on the Bible, and I'd taught the Epistle to the Galatians a dozen times. But I never understood St. Paul's lesson on law and freedom as much as I did when Hodge walked through my door and into his new life.

(40) Shakespearean Voices

Recently an English professor and I were watching a videotape of Nicolai's *The Merry Wives of Windsor*. He listened for a while, then observed, "I didn't know Falstaff could sing."

As a longtime opera-buff, I wasn't sure how to respond. Finally, I said, "You should hear Iago."

(41) Tipping God

The "Sound Off" column in the local paper is talking about tipping. A waitress called in to say "10 percent doesn't cut it any more." For good service, diners should tip 15 or even 20 percent. A woman responded with scripture. She said God only asks for 10 percent, and she wasn't going to give "some little waitress" more than she gives God. This led another reader to observe "God doesn't have to pay rent and utilities."

It's interesting to speculate about God's expenses. There must be some. I'm sure He lives in a nice part of town.

(42) Avoiding Sexist Language

A few years ago, working on my textbook *The Language of Argument*, I wrote an unacceptable sentence. Discussing credibility, I said, "You can never believe a woman when she talks about her ex-husband." I knew HarperCollins would jump all over that and reject it as sexist.

So I redid the sentence. I wrote, "You can never believe a person when he or she talks about his or her ex-spouse." This was politically correct, but barely English.

Finally I found the perfect line. I wrote, "You can never believe a man when he talks about his ex-wife." I knew this would pass editorial inspection. Nobody cares what you say about men.

(43) Visually Challenged in Gaza

Jud and I visited Gulf Shores last week and discussed a provocative issue: At what age does a man give up girl-watching? I said I didn't know, but I sure wasn't there yet. However, since I'm 68 and half-blind (one eye doesn't work; the other has tunnel vision), I see things a little different.

When I sat on the porch of the Pink Pony Pub with Jud and Cherie, healthy young girls strolled down by the water, but I couldn't see that far. Others walked further up on the sand, and I couldn't see them either, not from where I was sitting. I needed to stand up. Fortunately, my age gave me a plausible excuse. When the occasion was right, I could jump up, stomp my left leg, and complain about blood-circulation. This seemed reasonable, and people at adjacent tables looked on sympathetically.

Thereafter, whenever nature smiled on us, Jud or Cherie would ask, "Dan, how's your leg?" Immediately, I'd say, "Damn, it's getting constricted." Then I'd jump up, stare at the bikinis swinging by, and stomp my leg.

A young man sitting next to us asked, "Have you had that condition long?" "I've been suffering with it," I told him, "since puberty."

The problem of seeing pretty girls arose again when we went to eat, as we always do, at Hooters. (Man does not live by cheeseburgers alone.) Entering, we came indoors out of the bright sun, and I couldn't see anything. My friends had to help me to the table and find me a chair. In a minute or two, however, I could see better. The buxom waitress in orange shorts and a cut-off T-shirt brought menus to the table. On her T-shirt, she displayed a name-tag two-inches long and half-an-inch high. Jud and Cherie were whispering about my blindness when they heard me say, "*Michele?* You really spell that with one *l* ?" (A charming girl, she said she did and all other Michelles spelled their name wrong.) Then we ordered Rolling Rock and Hooterburgers. The meal was a rich success. I sat in a convenient chair and never once had to stand to stomp my leg.

Driving back to Mobile, Jud expressed a profound truth, one I'd like all my friends to remember. He said, "I'm not going to worry about your eyesight, Dan. Everytime I start to, I'm going to hear your voice saying, '*Michele?* You really spell that with one *l* ?' "

(44) The JCPenney Question

Riding up the escalator at JCPenney last month, I heard a girl talking to her mother in the department below me. The teenager was reading the size-label on a pair of jeans, and she asked, "How many inches is 24 inches?" Gliding upward, I felt better about things.

I'm older now, and there are a lot of questions I'll never find the answer to. (Why does the DNA molecule twist that way? What is "Bye, Bye, Miss American Pie" all about? Why doesn't Lois Lane recognize Superman?) I'll never understand all that. But some things — there are some things I know.

(45) Fielding the Easy Question

Let me tell you about the Catholic Social Services form Irene and I had to fill out in 1959. We were in Madison, Wisconsin, applying to adopt a baby. It was a challenge.

First we had to give pages of general information. We assured them we were healthy; we were affluent enough (I had just accepted a job-offer from Notre Dame); we had a solid marriage; and we were lifetime Catholics. Then came the question. It was printed on half of one line, and we had the other half of the line to answer it. (If we wrote tiny, we could crowd in a dozen words.) The form asked, "Why do you want a baby?"

I was frustrated. I felt the most honest answer was, "Dummy, we want a baby." Or "Why does anyone want a baby?" I wondered why they asked the question at all and why they didn't give us more room to answer it. Later I saw why. With more space, a childless couple might fill it with sentimental clichés. ("For years now, there has been an aching void in our hearts, and . . .") The agency didn't need that.

I knew I shouldn't sound cute or singular. We were facing a bureaucratic committee. (I imaged it having two priests, three nuns, and a mother of twelve.) We had to play it safe. Fortunately I'm good at that. Why did we want a baby? I wrote, "To love it, to teach it, and to enjoy it." This must have worked. Eleven months later, at a time when we were

43rd on the list of prospective parents, they gave us Molly. (And the angels sang!)

It helped that we were English teachers who could write pretty well. And it didn't hurt having that job at Notre Dame.

(46) See Professionals Communicate

The memo at my office read "Bob Sharp returned your call." It was a mistake, of course. Bob is a pediatrician who lives over in Fairhope. I hadn't called him. After lunch I rang his office. His secretary said he would be in Montgomery until Wednesday. She took my number. She said, "Dr. Sharp will get back to you."

(47) Sunday in the Park with Paul

In an Edinborough park behind the Sir Walter Scott monument are 50 or 60 benches. Each carries a memorial-plaque. Most say "In memory of my wife Anna who loved to feed the birds here" or "From John Harrison, an American who loved Scotland." One Sunday I was walking through the park enjoying the plaques, and I came on this one:

PAUL SHEEN
1962 - 1992
NO REGRETS

Sometimes poetry hits you in the face.

It's not hard to read the situation. Paul Sheen was a homosexual, an AIDS victim, and a brave and honest man. After I saw his memorial, I didn't read any others. I walked away thinking of his mortality and my own. As I left the park, I said what I say

#45 – "FIELDING THE EASY QUESTION"

again now: "God bless Paul Sheen. May he rest in peace."

(48) Adventures with Dooney & Bourke

Last year I found Irene at McRae's looking at some Dooney & Bourke handbags. They cost $200 or so, and she said, "I can't afford this."

Six months later at Flea Market Mobile, we found a huge display of Dooney & Bourke purses, all selling for $35. Irene said, "I don't want these; they are the fakes I read about. They're made in Korea." A week later, we learned that the flea-market had been raided by federal agents and the phony Dooney & Bourkes confiscated. They were violating trademark laws. Irene lamented, "I should have bought one. It would have been camp to own a phony Dooney & Bourke."

Last Saturday, Irene and I were at the market, and we saw a display of the same handbags. Now they were priced at $25, and the Dooney & Bourke logo was removed. Picking one up, Irene said, "I don't want this. It's not a Dooney & Bourke imitation. It's just a purse."

And that's the story. Irene didn't want the $200 purse and she didn't want the $25 purse. She didn't buy the real Dooney & Bourke. Then she rejected one handbag because it was a fake Dooney & Bourke, and another because it wasn't. I guess she doesn't need a purse.

(49) Let's Talk about Probability

The announcer on radio station WKRG gave a typical Mobile forecast, reporting "The chance of rain today is 80 percent." Then he added, "We'll see if that's right."

(50) Transubstantiation

My university colleague Marsha Dobson — a fashionably-dressed woman in her 50s — met me at the English Department coffee-pot one morning. I asked how she was, and she said, "Dan, I am *so goddamned mad*!" I asked what she was mad about. She said, "Transubstantiation." It was a rough way to start the day.

Transubstantiation, as you probably know, is the process by which bread and wine (in Christian belief) become the body and blood of Jesus Christ. I could imagine a person believing this or not believing it. But I didn't see how anyone could get mad about it. It turned out that, driving to school, Marsha had heard a news-report that the Anglican Church and the Roman Church were nearing agreement on this doctrine. She didn't like the ecumenical note.

When she left the room, I thought, "Nobody gets angry about Transubstantiation." I knew Marsha's husband was playing around and she had been having trouble with her son. That was probably the issue.

I think of this because I just heard 10 minutes of a call-in radio show. Two Mobile women were livid. One was mad because President Clinton smoked marijuana and had a girl-friend. The other was mad because his wife was heading up the health-care program. Hearing the rage and frustration, I knew there were sad lives out there. I muttered, "Nobody gets angry about Transubstantiation."

(51) Just Ask

Last week at Flea Market Mobile, a tradesman selling Russian memorabilia displayed an 8 x 10 inch sign saying "ASK ABOUT OUR LAY-AWAY PLAN." Since I'd never seen him there before and since many vendors don't show up every weekend, I was puzzled. I asked, "How does your lay-away plan work?" He said, "We don't have a lay-away plan."

(52) Let's Hear It for Trashy Bimbo

There's a new member in my family, one we talk about a lot. She's Trashy Bimbo, my next wife. (Notice that "Trashy" is a name.)

Trashy emerged as a contrast to the sane and healthy values Irene exhibits all the time. One day last month, when I suggested hot-dogs for lunch, Irene said, "Maybe your next wife will serve you hot-dogs"; then she came up with a broccoli casserole. That night when she complained of dog-hair and cat-hair on the rug, I told her my next wife would be near-sighted, and that wouldn't bother her. After a few such lines, Irene asked what kind of next wife I would look for. I assured her I wanted a trashy bimbo. (The name stuck.) Irene assumed Trashy would be a young thing, but I said "No way!" If she's under 20, I'm not interested.

As we describe her, Trashy has two goals: 1) to keep me happy so I'll leave her my money, and 2) to kill me off so she can get it sooner. Both goals offer me a wonderful life. Trashy and I will stay up late watching Showtime movies. We'll drink Wild Turkey and smoke Camel cigarettes. We'll make love a lot. We'll wake up to a house full of dirty glasses, messy ashtrays, dog-hair, cat-hair, *Playboy*, and *Cosmopolitan*. Breakfast will be coffee (never decaffeinated) and huge sweet-rolls. We'll eat most of our meals at Burger King, usually the double-cheeseburger and fries), but not all. Sometimes we'll have a Big Foot pizza delivered to the door. There will always be dessert, usually some form of chocolate. (Our candy-dish will overflow with bridge-mix.) We'll spend half our days down at Gulf Shores. We'll sit on the porch of the Pink Pony Pub, enjoying strangers, nachos, and Rolling Rock beer. Trashy and I will have an exciting marriage. My guess is it will last six weeks.

Now for the truth. Do I really want that kind of life when I already have a warm and handsome wife, a neat house, good books, healthy meals, regular hours, and a solid prospect of being healthy through my 70s? Well – maybe not. Not all the time anyway.

(53) Fast-Food Logic

This conversation took place at Wendy's last summer. I was talking to a serious young girl behind the food-counter

ME: I'll have the chicken-breast sandwich.

GIRL: You want that with everything?

ME: Yes.

GIRL: You want bacon on it?

ME: Yes, I'll have everything.

GIRL: Everything doesn't include bacon.

ME: It doesn't?

GIRL: No, that costs extra.

ME: Oh.

GIRL: Do you want bacon on your sandwich?

ME: No thanks. I'll just have everything.

(54) Locating Heaven and Hell

Recent issues of the *Weekly World News* had two
disturbing stories. One told of a Soviet engineering
team in western Siberia which drilled through into Hell.
They smelled smoke, heard the screams of the damned,
and prudently capped the hole. A second story showed
photos of Heaven taken from a space-probe. It is
located in the exact center of the Milky Way.

I worry about the condition of my soul when I
hear I am nine miles from Hell and 28,000 light-years
from Heaven.

(55) Say "I Don't Know"

Here's some good advice. When you're challenged with
a stupid question or an implicating question, say, "I
don't know." This always works.

Think of the messy conversations you can avoid
by turning off questions like these:

- Do you think Cher will get married again?
- Which is correct — ADD-ress or ad-DRESS?
- Do you think we're living in the last days
    prophesied in Revelation?
- Wouldn't Michael J. Fox be perfect as Hamlet?
- Is it true your ex-wife is moving back to town?

Such questions call for a two-part answer. First, you
say "I don't know." Then you shut up.

I used different forms of this response lately.
A student of mine asked me, in all seriousness, which
of the Rambo movies I preferred. I paused, then said,
"I couldn't say." Later, my Elderhostel friend Mary was
looking through some back-issues of *Newsweek* and
came on a story about Hugh Hefner and the Playboy
empire. Reading through it, she asked me, "What do

men see in these young girls anyway?"   I looked at
the magazine. I looked at a picture of Carrie Leigh,
Playmate of the Year.   I bit my lip and said, "I don't
know."

(56) <u>Ruth and "The Rest of the Story"</u>

What do you say to a girl-friend you haven't seen in
40 years?   Ruth Sampson visited us this weekend. She
was a beauty who thrilled my life in the late 40s and
early 50s.   She is still a beauty, a trim and gracious
lady of 60.

How could we begin a conversation?   Should I ask
"Did you have a nice life?"   Should I say "Tell me
about your marriage, your children, your work, your
city, your dreams"?   (People who meet like this should
send a resumé ahead.)   Once we got talking, however,
we didn't mention those things. We talked about
people we remembered. We were back in high-school
gossiping about our friends.

The news was mixed.   Bob Ibinger got rich. Donn
Waldum married an English girl and is retired
someplace in California.   Sverre Tinglum had a problem
with alcohol but got over it. Donna Quackenbush died,
and her husband married Shiela Hansen.   Tom
Shoemaker died, and his wife went to Alaska with
Norman Rozmanowski. Bob Huntley is still teaching in
Virginia, but he and Jill broke up. Calvin Clark died
well; he and his girl-friend were on a hunting-trip in
Canada when a coronary got him. Jim Phillips died
badly, a long bout with cancer. Farreol Watson killed
himself, and nobody knows why. Howard Boyer made
a lot of money and has a big house in Minneapolis.
Royal Roberts . . . .   Ruth and I talked for two hours;

we were doing Paul Harvey's "The Rest of the Story."
All in all, it was a good story.

A strange moment occurred at Sunday Mass.
During the Rite of Peace (where people embrace and
shake hands and say "The peace of Christ be with
you"), I hugged Ruth who was standing beside me.
Then I reached across her to embrace Irene, and
somehow we – the three of us – spontaneously hugged
together. *Wham!* Right then, a lot of time-sequences
clanged together. Teenage Danny was hugging his girl-
friend; Dr. McDonald was embracing his wife; and we
were all part of a 2000-year-old ceremony. This
wasn't "The Rest of the Story"; it was the whole story.
It was *my* story.

I don't pretend this was a mystic experience. I
didn't hear the music of the spheres or see the hand
of God. But it was an incredible, unifying moment. I
will never forget that hug.

(57) There's Always Plan B

Nationality accounts for a lot. Irene claims she never
understood me until we visited Ireland. She said, "Dan,
they're all like you." (Meaning, I guess, they're pleasant
and irresponsible.) Irene is Russian. Russians expect
the worst to happen. When the first snowflake falls,
they moan, "Oh, God, it's here. The Ice Age."

Irene always expects trouble. What if I go blind
and she can't drive us around? What if the computer
won't take her disk? What if the plane is late? What
if . . . Lately, I've found a phrase that soothes her. I
say, "Don't worry. There's always a Plan B."

I'm glad everyone doesn't live so prudently. I
was impressed in St. Croix when Molly and Ed were
planning to be married on a large, open sailboat.

#52 - "LET'S HEAR IT FOR TRASHY BIMBO"

There'd be 40 people aboard, all dressed up for the ceremony. I asked Ed, "What if it rains? What is Plan B?" He shrugged, "Plan B is we get wet."

(58) Wallowing

One of the joys of being an English teacher is that student-lines stay with you for years. I remember the freshman boy who described Viet Nam atrocities. One soldier, he wrote, was put in a tiny cell and just left there: "He had to wallow in his own increment."

Hey, that's my retirement goal. I plan to fly to Vegas, eat filet mignon, drink Wild Turkey, look at the show-girls, play some blackjack — and just wallow in my own increment.

(59) The Play's the Thing

Because I've appeared in a few plays, I sometimes have the actor's nightmare. I dream I'm on stage (often in something by Noel Coward) and I can't remember any lines. The leading-lady asks me what time it is, and I don't know. She prompts me saying, "Did you know it's after two?" I stammer, "Y-yes." She asks why I was out so late, and I have no idea. There is a long pause, and I'm miserable. Then I wake up.

Lately, I've gotten smarter. When the leading-lady asks where I was, I remember I'm only dreaming. It's not a real play. *Any answer I give will be OK.* So with full dramatic emphasis, I say, "I went [pause] to see Monica." The scene can go on as long as it likes, and I never miss a line. It's great.

I have now taken my show on the road. Sometimes when I'm talking to the people at my office, I pretend I'm in a play. And whenever they speak to me, I answer with dramatic intensity. Yesterday, Christie, our receptionist, stopped me when I arrived and said I had a phone-call from New York. I assumed a tragic tone. "Yes," I said, "I *knew* it was coming." When the pretty administrator across the hall smiled in my doorway and asked if I was having a nice day, I didn't say, "Yeah, how about you?" I gave her a brave smile. "Debbie," I said, "they've asked me not to talk about that." (She nodded and backed out of the room.) When the mail-clerk said "No letters today, Doctor," I gasped, "Thank God!" When Jud phoned and asked if we could have a beer at 4:00, I gave him a full 10-second pause. Then I said, "Would you mind repeating the question?" I was in good form yesterday. The play went great.

You might want to try this. Pretend your morning is part of a play, everyone around you is your supporting cast, and all your lines are crucial dialogue. Say them that way. Probably no one will notice, and nobody will mind. Anyone who thinks you're weird probably thought that already. And you can enjoy yourself. You can be what you always knew you were. You're the star.

(60) What You See Is What You Get

David Luis' *Fascinating Facts* (1976) celebrates human perception. It says, "On a clear night, when there is no moon, a person sitting on a mountain peak can see a match struck 50 miles away."

I imagine Irene on that dark mountaintop. She will see the flicker of light 50 miles in the distance. Immediately she'll cough and fan the air. She'll protest, "They shouldn't allow smoking in here."

(61) I Love You, Therefore. . .

As an author who writes books on logic, I must tell
you about two ads that are keeping me awake nights.
Both say, "If you really love someone, you'll use our
product."

The first sells Omega watches. It shows a
handsome couple conversing in a sports-car and has the
caption: "Some people need only one man. Or one
woman. Or one watch." Where does a logician go from
there?

I start with the fact I own three watches. I use
my Rolex to impress people. I wear a Hamilton replica
for everyday. And I take a plastic, Radio Shack model
when I knock around at the Gulf. Does it follow I
need three men – and three women? Yes, I guess it
does. Only I need four men. My best friends –
Charley, Larry, Jud, and Mike – are central to my
experience. (Each is mad in a different way, so I
couldn't lose any of them.) And – in my fantasy
world anyway – I require three women. I need Susan
Lucci to impress people. I want Irene for everyday.
And I'd like Mandy Somebody (a blond cheerleader) to
drink beer with me at the beach. What kind of
argument can I make out of that?

Lying awake last night, I imagined a 10-second TV
spot showing Mandy and me sitting on the porch at
the Pink Pony Pub. She's wearing a white sun-hat and
a broad smile; I'm in my Hawaiian shirt with a plastic
wristwatch. Our table is littered with beer-cans. The
deep-voiced announcer says: "Some people need only
four men. And three women. And three watches."
Over this comes the printed message: "Vote McDonald
for U.S. Senator." Who knows, that might work.

The second ad sells Emeraude perfume. It shows an elegant couple, maybe in their thirties. He's in the background; the focus is on her. She says: "I love only one man. I wear only one fragrance." Of course, I lie in bed speculating about this.

How might the argument relate to me? The truth doesn't seem promising. I'd have to admit, "I've loved one woman for 40 years. I don't wear fragrance at all." Even "I love Irene. I wash with Ivory Soap" isn't very compelling. Finally, since the Emeraude ad is so exclusively feminine, I came up with a male variation. This one rings true: "I love only one dog. I drink only Coors, Michelob, Budweiser, Löwenbräu, Rolling Rock, Corona, Red Stripe, Red Dog, Molson, Moosehead, Heineken, and Miller Genuine Draft."

I'm still working on that Emeraude ad. What cause-effect arguments can I devise beginning "I love my Macintosh, therefore..."? Or "I lust after Elaine Faulkner, so..."? Or "I adore Verdi, consequently..."? Man, I may never get to sleep.

(62) Poor Dan

I guess it's time for pity. I've been two-thirds blind for a year or so now, and I've managed to live with it. I can barely read; I don't drive any more; and when I drop something, it disappears from the universe. Still, I stay upbeat. I don't complain. Yesterday, however, a sad event occurred.

We were having the Bahrs over for a spaghetti supper, and I went to K&B to get some beer. I found Corona on sale for $4.99, so I bought two 6-packs. It wasn't till I got home I saw I'd bought Corona Light. Damn! I didn't see the word "Light." To make matters worse, Bob and Alice turned out to be wine-drinkers, so I'm stuck with a dozen bottles of light beer. *Light beer!* I don't know what I'm going to do with it.

I think it's time for you people out there to moan and commiserate and say, "Poor Dan. He's blind. He has a hard life."

(63) Laying Out the Big Bucks

In recent years, Irene and I have traveled in England and in Italy. She's more comfortable shopping in England.

In London, we bought things paying pounds. Each pound was worth $1.50, so something selling for $10 was marked "6.67." It seemed inexpensive. In Venice, we spent lira, and each lira was worth 1/1500 of a dollar. That $10 item was offered for "15,000." Irene wouldn't spend 15,000 on anything she couldn't drive away.

But I would. I bought her an elegant golden pin with an emerald-green stone. Whenever she wears it, I announce, "Isn't that lovely? I laid out twenty thousand for that." When listeners exclaim, "You spent twenty thousand..." – I cut them off. Standing tall, I say, "Yes, it's a lot. But Irene has been a good wife for 40 years. She deserves something special."

(64) Saint Daniel of Mobile

In a provocative tabloid-ad, the American Life Church says it feels there are many saints on earth today who have not been recognized. Therefore, if you send them $5, they will declare you a saint. You get a certificate announcing your canonization.

As a Catholic, I am intrigued by this. How would I behave if I were a saint? Would I give my goods to the poor? Would I buy a Buick Park Avenue? Would I send for a vanity license-plate that says "ST. DAN"? Should I mention the new title on my resumé? Would it go under "Awards" or "Highest Degree Attained"?

How would I break the news to Archbishop Lipscomb? I have a fantasy of phoning the archdiocese and asking to speak to him. The secretary will say, "Who is calling please?" I'll let that hang in the air for 10 seconds, then I'll say "Saint Daniel of Mobile." That should shake them up down at the Cathedral.

(65) "Raharah?"

Here's a term that will help you deal with your world. It says, "There is a choice item here, but only one. I'm going to take it."

The phrase derived from family life at the McDonald house. Sometimes at the dinner-table, there would be one slab of cheese left or one piece of cake. The kids would like to just grab it, but Irene taught them manners. She said, "Before you take the last piece of anything, ask others at the table, 'Would anyone like to share this?'"

The kids were dutiful; they always asked the question. But it came out in strange forms. At first it was "Wouldyoulikesharethis?" Then it became "Ooairiss?" and "Rariss?" Finally it metamorphosed into a whispered "Raharah?" Having asked the question, they helped themselves to whatever they wanted.

You should find the phrase useful. Occasionally, you'll ride with a group and someone has to take that front seat. At a banquet, you'll see the best table is by the window. Opening a refrigerator, you may find a six-pack of Budweiser and one bottle of Heineken. As a civil person, you can't just take that choice item.

So first you whisper "Raharah?" and then grab it.
Courtesy is a wonderful thing.

(66) We All Need Heroes

On her M.A. English exam five years ago, a woman
described the typical hero of Restoration comedy. She
wrote, "He is a complete rake. He is unfaithful before,
during, and after the marriage ceremony." That
"during" impresses me. Some men I may not approve
of, but I'd like to shake their hand.

(67) A Blind Man at *The Piano*

Last Sunday Irene and I and the Harwells went to see
the award-winning movie *The Piano*. With my
glaucoma and tunnel-vision, I couldn't make much of it.
I saw a lot of darkness, some bright splashes of color,
and things moving around. (There weren't many well-
lit, stationary scenes.) When we walked out, I was
told I had missed seeing the nude wife with her lover
and the enraged husband chopping off her finger. I
said I didn't mind missing that.

 I told them I could follow some scenes by their
sound. I enjoyed the music, and I knew when the
couple was making love by the grunting and moaning.
Charley told me, "That wasn't passion, Dan. That was
six Mauri savages carrying a piano through a swamp."

 "Yeah," I said, "I always get those two mixed up."

(68) Photographic Evidence

As one who writes books about argument and
persuasion. I love to see solid photographic evidence.
(A definitive instance is that picture of Patty Hearst
holding a gun during the bank-robbery.) Two recent
tabloid stories offer provocative examples.

#65 - "RAHARAH?"

The *National Enquirer* tells of Monica Nieto, a Spanish teenager who can bend forks and spoons with the power of her mind. Should you doubt this, it shows a photo of her holding a bent fork.

Equally impressive is the *Weekly World News* story of a ghost who invaded a wedding in Romiley, England. Guests reported a short, cigar-smoking stranger who appeared at the ceremony and the reception – and then disappeared. They know he was a ghost because he didn't show up on the wedding-pictures. The tabloid published two large photos, and very clearly – on both of them – the stranger isn't there.

Hey, I know conclusive evidence when I see it.

(69) Enjoying Trivia

Have you seen all the books and newspapers offering "Trivia"? I love them.

Tabloid columns tell me that Cleopatra married her brother and that boys sleep 10 minutes a night longer than girls. Books like *Fascinating Facts* report that Eskimos don't gamble, and Attila the Hun was a dwarf. Other sources assure me that flies prefer to breed in the center of a room, and there are 9,000,000 rats in New York City. When I go to bed, I can know I'll be taller when I get up in the morning.

Why learn all this? The *Weekly World News* justified its "Trivia Treasure Chest," saying we need to stay competitive:

"Getting tired of that brother-in-law or
friend at work who thinks he knows
everything? You don't have to put up
with these maddening know-it-alls. Here are

some fascinating facts that even the most knowledgeable expert might not know."

So it's all oneupmanship. If you sit at your desk and casually observe "Nobody knows where Mozart is buried," you've scored five points.

I can go the *News* one better. I can give you facts that no one around you will know. Consider these:

- Two-thirds of the centerfold girls in *Playboy* are 5'4" or shorter.
- The most misspelled word in English is "accommodate."
- American League ballplayers hit 9 points above their usual batting-average when playing on their birthday.
- French designer Coco Chanel insisted that fat women should never wear white.
- The average visitor to a Mississippi casino goes home losing $113. (For this, however, the gambler usually gets dinner and a few drinks.)
- Vegetarians are most likely to eat meat at Easter.
- In a 1993 poll, Midwest film-critics chose *Citizen Kane* as the best American movie ever made. Second best was *Butch Cassidy and the Sundance Kid*.

How can I be sure no expert, no trivia-buff, will know these things? That's easy. I made them up. (Don't they sound plausible?)

I suspect many of the facts in the trivia-books are made up. "Eskimos don't gamble"? "Nine million rats in New York City"? Come on.

It's fun when you start to create facts. There I am, walking through Bel Air Mall, looking casual and mature. And I'm thinking. I'm muttering to myself. I'm saying: "Left-handed women shouldn't eat chili" – "George Washington's mother weighed 260 pounds" – "Italians dream in color" – "The average highway patrolman has an IQ of 108" – "Alexander the Great had no navel." Hey, I'm enjoying myself. What do you think about walking through the mall?

(70) Brothers

Sometimes you make a friend almost instantly. This morning, I went to the Mobile Eye, Ear, Nose and Throat Clinic to see Dr. Ball about having a cataract removed. When I came in, I was directed to the second floor. I entered the elevator with a distinguished-looking man in his 60s. He wore a suit so I thought he might be a doctor. In the darkened elevator, I had to ask for help. "I'm sorry," I said, "but I can't see the buttons in here. Would you please press the button for the second floor?" The man said, "What?"

We were laughing about this exchange when the door opened. Outside the elevator, we shook hands. The man pointed me toward the Eye Desk, and I yelled, "Take it easy."

(71) No Double-Talk, Please

Irene and I just came from St. Ignatius where Father Harmless lectured us on the divinity-humanity of Jesus. I waited for the usual double-talk. It never came.

The problem is easily stated. The gospel says Jesus wept for Lazarus, and then raised him from the dead. Weeping is a human act; raising the dead is divine. Was Jesus human or divine or some combination? And what kind of combination? Was he schizophrenic, a split-personality? With his human nature, could he lust after Mary Magdalene? With his divine nature, was he really an embodied spirit, an all-knowing god masquerading as human? If Jesus knew he was going to raise Lazarus, was he faking when he wept for him? Did he feel the pains of crucifixion?

Father Harmless was brilliant. He sketched the whole fifth-century debate. He didn't resort to easy analogies. (Jesus was a mixture of human and divine, which blended perfectly, like water and wine.) He said most heresies are a form of oversimplification, sloganizing, what he called "the Dan Quayle school of theology." He said we, as Catholics, have to believe Jesus was true god and true man and *one* person. He said it's interesting to discuss the issue, but it will remain a mystery.

Hey, that's what I thought. As a teacher, I have always been impatient with cop-out, semantic "explanations." So I can't understand the Incarnation — big deal! I live with Irene and a white tomcat and a copy of *The Double Helix*. One more mystery isn't going to bother me.

(72) Salt-Free Living

Irene just read the latest issue of *The Johns Hopkins Medical Letter: Health After 50*, and I see bleak days ahead.

An article was titled "Why Everyone Should Cut Back on Sodium." It said that humans need only 200 milligrams of sodium daily, and Americans are taking in 3000-4000. This can lead to hypertension, heart disease, and forms of cancer. On reading this, Irene ran to our kitchen cupboard and pulled out boxes and cans and checked their sodium content. With the exception of a box of Nabisco Shredded Wheat, *everything* had way too much salt. She thought about this all day and after supper made her health announcement.

We can live very well, she said, if we avoid ham, hamburger, hot dogs, any kind of deli meat, pizza, and chili. Also, canned or frozen soup, biscuits, breakfast-rolls, grilled-cheese sandwiches, and anything else with cheese. As well as cold cereal (except Shredded Wheat), peanuts, chips, french-fries, ice cream, salad-dressing, ketchup, mustard, and pickles. And, of course, anything at all from McDonald's or Burger King.

I asked what we *were* going to eat, and she said fresh fruits and vegetables and Shredded Wheat. I reminded her that recent taste-tests established that only 15 percent of Americans can distinguish Shredded Wheat from the box it came in. Irene ignored me and insisted, "This is how we have to live from now on."

As she left the room, I said all a civilized husband could say. I muttered, "*Bon appetit.*"

(73) Unleashing Cosmic Power

In *Armchair in Hell*, detective Pete Chambers describes a current girl-friend. He says, "Some women might say Lola was heavy. Some women might say she was top-heavy. But a man wouldn't say one damn thing." (It's great being an English professor; you can quote literature.)

I think of this because I just saw a "Call a Psychic" ad in the *Weekly World News*. It shows a top-heavy brunette, generously revealed and leaning into the camera. The caption reads, "My Psychic Told Me How to Unleash My Power." This makes a man think.

I imagine the girl sitting at home, feeling inadequate and wondering if she should make the call. Then she dials Mystic Marketing (1-900-737-3726) and pays $3.49 a minute to explain her problems to a psychic. I see him poring over his astrological tables, computing the stars in ascendance, correcting for planetary interference, and tuning in to the cosmic wisdom of the universe. Then he tells her, "Unhook the top four buttons on your blouse."

To paraphrase *Hamlet*, "There needs no ghost come from the grave to tell her that." But I'm glad somebody did.

(74) Beethoven's Sixth

I have friends who worry about me and ask what I'm going to do during my retirement. A good answer is to tell them what I did Wednesday night.

From 8:00, I saw on my screened-in patio and listened to the Chicago Symphony. I heard Daniel Barenboim conducting Beethoven's Sixth (the Pastoral Symphony). I sat in the dark; the weather was cool. At my feet lay Boswell, my golden retriever. In my lap sat Hodge, a large, white tomcat. At my right hand was a cold Heineken.

Friends, I'm doing all right in my retirement. You take care of yourself.

(75) "Other Restrictions May Apply"

I love the car-leasing and car-rental ads. The headlines boast you can get a lush automobile at an inexpensive rate. They show a gleaming car. They urge you to call an 800-number or see your local dealer. Then at the bottom of the page is an inch-and-a-half of tiny print. It says, in effect, that some people can get that bargain rate – but you can't.

If I were young again, I'd use this system with all my love-letters. The message would be "I love you, sweetheart. I want you to marry me." Then, at the bottom of the page, the small print:

> "No purchase necessary. Restrictions will occur in some areas. Terms may vary. Offer subject to state and local regulations and regional availability. Offer void if taxed or prohibited. Quantities are limited. Not available after September 30. Other restrictions may apply. Have a nice day."

(76) Life in Heaven

An article in the *National Examiner* describes the afterlife. Doris Stokes, a London psychic now deceased, sends back word that Heaven is lovely. It has grassy parks, theaters, schools, and concert-halls. This is reassuring, but I have questions.

I wonder who mows the grass. What movies are showing at the theaters? Are they all G-rated? Are the schools Catholic schools? Do they have a placement-office? Who's playing at the concert-halls – Mozart? Elvis? The Music of the Spheres?

A number of tabloid stories assure us there is romance in Heaven. Rita Hayworth and Orson Wells are together again. Elvis is married to Natalie Wood. I think about this. Heaven will have Nell Gwyn, Elizabeth Siddal, Evelyn Nesbit, Ann Sheridan, and other

#76 - "LIFE IN HEAVEN"

beauties who are young again. I've been happy with Irene, but you know how it is. I'm reminding her our contract is "till death do us part."

(77) Remembering Names

After 60, my memory began to fade, so I've worked out a remembering-system. Last night I tried to teach it to my son. We had just met a lady named Naomi, who wore a huge pile of black hair. I said, "Nick, you can use her hair to tell you her name." I said he should see the hair, ask himself "Do I like it?" and answer "Nay." He can think of "hair" and "nay," "hair" and "nay," "hair" and "Naomi."

That is a neat system, but Nick wasn't impressed. He said, "Dad, I'd rather do it the hard way."

(78) Beautiful Women

I love talking to pretty girls, and lately I've been doing a fair amount of it. It helps to be older and half-blind.

Every six or eight weeks, I call Minneapolis and talk to Ruth Sampson. (This is her maiden name. She has had a married name for 40-plus years, but I don't recognize that.) Ruthie was a teenager who electrified my youth (circa 1950), and it's great to keep in touch with her. We discuss everything — the current news, her latest travels, those grandchildren, etc. — but we also talk about old times, about the good life in postwar Wisconsin. We recall swimming in Black River, drinking Blatz beer at Castle Hill, cruising in my '53 Chevy (she taught me to drive), and meeting friends at the Jackson County Fair. ("What ever happened to Bob Huntley?") We aren't neurotics clinging to the past. We're good friends sharing happy memories.

I saw Ruth three years ago, and she is a handsome, civilized lady. But I don't think of her that way, not during the phone-conversations. In our last call, I told her, "You know, Ruthie, when I talk to you, I still see you as an 18-year-old girl." This startled her a bit, and there was a short pause. Then she laughed. She said, "I can live with that."

My current semi-blindness produced a comparable scene here in Mobile. Last Thursday, I walked into Building 2001 at Brookley and met Carolyn Dunnam. (She is the keen lady who heads up our Elderhostel programs.) Looking into her office, I said, "Carolyn, I just came out of the bright sun, and everything in here seems pitch-black." Immediately, she announced, "Then I have to tell you the news. You may not know that I've lost 40 pounds. I've had my breasts enlarged, and my hair has turned blond." She laughed, "What do you think of that?" My answer came from the heart. Staring into the darkness, I said, "I think I'm in love."

(79) Perfection City

It was a rare morning. Eight years ago, I drove over to the Grand Hotel to do a program on technical writing for Scott Paper engineers. I left early in the Cutlass Ciera I'd bought a week before. It smelled new. I got out in the hotel parking-lot and walked toward the entrance. I looked good. I'd had a haircut the preceding day, and I was freshly shaved. I was wearing my new blue suit with a white shirt and maroon tie. My shoes reflected the morning sun. At the entrance of the luxury hotel, a uniformed black man held the door for me. He said "Good morning" and asked how I felt. I said "Great" and asked how he felt. We were civilized. As I walked through the lobby, full of fresh flowers, two ladies behind the desk greeted me and asked how things were going. I said "Fine, thank you."

I noticed on my Rolex (just six months old) it was only 7:30. I had time for breakfast before going to my program. At the door of the dining-room, I met the hostess, a slim 20-year-old with long black hair and a white dress. She identified herself as Susan and inquired how I was this morning. As she led me into the room, she asked, "Would a table by the window be all right?" I said that would be wonderful. She said, "Your server today is Melanie. She will be with you in a minute. Can I get you a cup of coffee while you wait?" "Fine," I said, "I'll have it black."

I watched her walk away, then leaned back. I looked out over the broad expanse of green lawn and Mobile Bay shining in the distance. It was perfect − it was all perfect. I reflected, "Sometimes a man gets what he deserves."

(80) "Dear, We Have to Talk"

At the last meeting of the Executive Committee of the Gulf Coast Humanities Consortium, we found 100 percent agreement on an important social issue. We discussed the best way to answer when a wife says, "Dear, we have to talk."

We agreed the most honest response would be, "Of course, darling. First let me stop in the bathroom. I want to slash my wrists."

(81) Ratihabition in Mobile

Why was I sitting home Thursday night feeling palpebral, cavernicolous, and frigorific? Why was I experiencing escamotage, anemometry, and armigerous coaration? You can guess why. I was preparing for a spelling-bee.

The adventure began two weeks ago when Nancy Hanna phoned Irene and told her about the Literacy Council's annual spelling-bee. She said Compass Bank, her employer, wanted to field a team this year. (Players would be called the Compass Points.) She already had two volunteers, but she still needed one player and one alternate. With the generosity that has made her a legend, Irene volunteered me as the player and herself as the alternate.

I was willing to go along with this. I spell pretty well. I had qualms, however, when the mail brought us the "GGLC Spelling Bee Word Study List - 1995." This offered five typed pages, each with four columns containing 50 words — about 1000 words altogether. On each page, the first column had "Simpler" words ("cosmetic," "tapestry"); the second had "Intermediate" words ("onerous," "parietal"). The third column was headed "Advanced," and the fourth, "Additional." I would have called them "Forget it!" There I saw "kaumographer" and "tsunami," and when I concentrated, strange words began to swim around on the page.

As I worked through the lists, I did some panicky thinking. I thought, "I've spent 50 years letting people believe I know things; now they'll see the truth." I even flirted with a plausible excuse. When I misspelled a word, I could say, "I'm sorry, I've been taking Lortab to ease leg-pain. It clouds my memory." I might add, "Who'd think battlefield shrapnel would pain a man 50 years later?" Nobody would scorn a wounded veteran.

As it turned out, I didn't need the excuse. The Compass Points won the spelling-bee. Irene was pressed into service, and she was brilliant. Nancy Hanna got a huge plaque to show off at Compass Bank for the next year. Irene and I and a bright girl named Lori won silver trophies. It was a lovely moment. I felt eclectic, and grandiloquent, and even a bit megalomaniacal.

Nancy says we'll have to go back next year to defend our championship. Hey, I'm ready.

(82) The Language of Civility

In her efforts to raise our kids right, Irene gave them a civilizing rule. She said, "Before you say anything about a person, ask yourself: Is it kind? Is it necessary? And is it true?" That was good counsel, but it didn't curb Nicholas.

At supper one night — the children were in their early teens — Molly (the oldest) was being a bit imperious. Finally, her sister (the youngest) called her "a bitch." And Nicholas was quick to speak up for Molly. "You shouldn't say that, Becky," he said. "That's not kind or necessary."

(83) Holistic Medicine at the McDonald House

Sometimes the papers bring good news. I learned this morning from the *Mobile Register* — quoting the Associated Press, the *Journal of the American Medical Association*, and Dr. Paul Ridker of the Harvard Medical School — that drinking beer is good for me. I can't argue with authorities like that.

Specifically, a new report says that alcohol-consumption is directly linked to increased levels of an enzyme, t-PA, that helps break down blood-clots. This reduces the risk of heart attack.

I'm spreading the news at my house. Tonight before supper when I reached for a Budweiser, I told Irene, "Don't worry, Honey, I'm taking care of myself." When I opened a second beer, I assured her, "I'm

#83 - "HOLISTIC MEDICINE"

fighting blood-clots all the time." After the meal, I grabbed another beer and retired to watch the Dallas-Detroit game. Holding up the bottle, I announced, "This one's for public health." And at half-time, I went to the kitchen for a beer and a snack. Walking by Irene with my fourth Budweiser and a dish of cheese and crackers, I told her, "A man's got to take care of his heart."

Irene was philosophical. I heard her mutter, "A man's gotta do what a man's gotta do."

(84) Dealing with Conservatives

Some of my best friends are conservatives, and I try to be nice to them. It isn't always easy.

I hear strange opinions. My next-door neighbor thinks we should round up all the homeless (and most Haitians and homosexuals) and lock them in prison. (To pay for this, he's willing to have his taxes raised .000005 percent.) A university colleague thinks we should send out the U.S. Air Force and bomb Serbs, Iraqis, North Koreans, and other brown-skinned people. A lady I talk to at church has a unique health-care program. It would require doctors to make house-calls, but only to houses valued at $180,000.

Years ago, Grandma McCredden taught me a prayer which sums up the conservative position. It goes: "God bless me and my wife. My son John and his wife. Us four. No more. Amen."

The problem is my conservative friends are genuinely nice people. They just don't see far outside their estate. An Elderhostel friend (I'll call her Carla) is a charming Southern lady. But she was distressed by social programs. One July noon, she was driving a few of us to the Country Club for lunch. We were cruising along I-65 in her Lincoln Continental. On the side of the road were a dozen convicts picking up trash in the 95-degree heat. Carla was protesting a new Civil Rights proposal, and she gestured toward the black prisoners. "What I want to know," she said, *without a hint of irony*, "is what do these people want?"

(85) Subjective Numbers

My wife went to the doctor last week, and found herself being weighed and measured by a young Southern girl. It was her first day on the job. The girl tried to take Irene's height, but couldn't get the measuring-bar to stay in place. Finally, in frustration, she asked, "Mrs. McDonald, how tall are you?" Irene told her 5'8" and she wrote that down. Then she put Irene on the scale and announced her weight as 141 pounds. Irene protested this was five pounds too heavy. That was Christmas weight she'd lose in a week or two. The girl asked "Is 136 about right?" Irene said yes, and that was recorded on her medical-chart.

When she told me about this, I remembered the words of the parable: "What do you owe my master?" "100 measures of wheat." "Take thy bill and write 80." Anyway, Irene is very happy with her new statistics. She told me, "If I lose 10 more pounds, I'll be down to my drivers-license weight."

(86) Marriage Power

The cover of a recent *Weekly World News* announced a medical breakthrough – a cure for impotence. (The story inside celebrated a pill called Vigorex Forte, something made from green oats.) The line on the cover that caught my attention said, "Put Pizzazz Back in Your Marriage!" I found this compelling, but only because I have glaucoma and have lost my peripheral eyesight. With tunnel-vision, I see only parts of words. I read "Put Pizza Back in Your Marriage!" This makes sense to me. My love life is in good shape, but I could use a lot more pizza.

(87) Secrets from the Past

Think about this. My mother-in-law (an old-country lady with keen insights) was looking at some family photographs. One was of Joe O'Mara, her daughter Betty's husband, who is now deceased. As long as I knew him, Joe was bald. Grandma picked up an old picture and said, "Here's one of Joe back when he had hair. Wasn't he handsome?" Then she added, "I wonder if we knew it then."

OK, senior citizen, look at your old photos. Were you beautiful? Were you handsome back then? Did anybody notice? Why didn't they say something?

(88) What Price Gentility?

Irene keeps a beautiful house, and I rejoice to live in it. But a lot of places are off-limits.

We have a handsome living-room we visit once a week, and an elegant dining-room we use almost every month. Both are tastefully appointed with paintings, some nice antiques, and (usually) fresh flowers. I am instructed to keep the dog and the cat out of those rooms and to avoid them myself unless I'm on official business and my passport is in order. I don't mind this. I enjoy living with handsome surroundings, even if I never see them.

The problem is our two bathrooms. The front one has green print wallpaper, white wicker accessories, a beige-knit toilet-seat cover, three finger-tip towels (they're white with green embroidery), an antique soap-dish containing a bar of expensive rose-color soap, and (usually) fresh flowers. My instructions are to stay the hell out of the front bathroom.

I can live with this. The bathroom I use has a big bar of Ivory soap, a good-sized handtowel on the rack by the sink, and an old, blue bathtowel hanging over the shower-rod. Back there, hygiene is possible. But I see trouble coming. On Monday, Irene asked me if I could take the bathtowel from the rod (where "people might see it") and hang it on the rack behind the shower-curtain. (Whoever these "people" are, we don't want them thinking anyone in our house takes a shower and dries off with a big towel.) On Wednesday, I noticed that my handtowel by the sink had been replaced by three baby towels. (They are lovely. The middle one is rose, and the other two are mauve, I think.) So now, after I wash my hands, I have to reach behind the shower-curtain to dry them. And then yesterday, I found my bathtowel behind the curtain had been replaced by an elegant handtowel. It is 14" x 22" and has a bluish design which exactly matches our wallpaper.

So where am I now? As I see it, I can enjoy elegant living and a happy marriage if I never use either bathroom. So I'm working out a system. I can take showers up at the university gym. I can keep a secret towel in one of the bathroom cupboards and hope Irene never finds it. And I expect to be seeing a lot of Mr. McKelvaine. He is the affable man who owns the Shell station down on the corner.

(89) Bikinis in the *News*

There are lots of reasons to buy the *Weekly World News*, and one is it's always the swimsuit issue.

Every week, it prints half a dozen bikini-photos and makes no effort to pass them off as news. The caption usually reads, "Shapely Sharon McBride came to Hollywood from Tomah, Wisconsin, where she led the high-school cheerleading team. She wants to hit it big in show-business, and she's off to a good start. Already she's been seen on *Matlock*."

I don't object to this. I think pretty-girl photos would do a lot for *College English* and *PMLA*, the academic journals I had to read over the years. If I see an article titled "The Titular Dilemma: Henry Miller and the Neo-Horatian Syndrome," I'd like to find it next to a picture of Binky Williams, a gymnast from Fort Lauderdale.

One recent photo did have news value. It shows Toni Anne Wyner protesting a law banning nudity on Florida beaches. She is holding a copy of the Bill of Rights over her naked body. I gave the picture to a university colleague, and he was much impressed. He said, "It makes you proud to be an American."

(90) Resumé Truth

Ten years ago, I appeared in court as an expert-witness. It was a Bible/First Amendment/school case, and I had published a book on argument and a book on scripture. The lawyer put me on the stand and tried to establish my credibility. First, he handed me a document and said, "Is this your resumé?" I said it was, and he had it admitted into evidence. Then I panicked. Suppose he followed up. Suppose he asked, "Is this an honest statement of your professional work?"

I'd be under oath. I'd have to say, "No, that's my resumé." Fortunately, the question never came.

(91) "You Wanna Ride in My Space-Ship?"

According to a story in the *Weekly World News*, a young man in Bogota, Colombia, put on green makeup and a glittery green outfit and posed as a space-alien. He seduced 25 girls by promising them rides in his space-ship. This bothers me.

Where were those stupid women when I was growing up?

(92) Two Useful Lines

Some lines stay with you forever.

When I graduated from Black River Falls High School (we're talking pre-history now), we heard Pastor Tollefson give our baccalaureate address. In it, he pinpointed the exact moment when evil entered the world: One morning a caveman walked down to the river and looked at his face in the water. He said to himself, "I want more cows." If this doesn't make much sense today, let me assure you it didn't in 1945 either. Nevertheless, the line has stayed with me. Occasionally, I see a red BMW or a neighbor's wife or Truman Capote's prose – and I get envious. I mutter, "*I want more cows*."

Last year on the Bullwinkle cartoon show, I found a new line. The Russian villain – Boris Badanov – was threatening some evil deed. Bullwinkle the moose protested, "You can't do that. That's dirty pool." Illustrating his depraved charm, Badanov asked, "Is other kind pool?" I'm finding a lot of use for that question. Last week, Irene said, "These brussels-sprouts taste funny." On Sunday, she complained, "The deacon's sermon was pointless today." This noon watching *All My Children*, she pointed to one character and said, "That's the man who's cheating on his wife." Routinely I think, "*Is other kind pool?*"

(93) Heirs to the Kingdom

On WMOB, I hear Sister Gloria, an evangelist from Plantation, Florida. She has an intense ministry with a singular name. She remembers that followers of Jesus are not servants or strangers; they are "*heirs*" of the promise." Also, they are leaders in the new world order. They are "the *head* and not the tail." Each Christian is an heir; each is a head . So Sister Gloria calls her ministry "Heir-Heads for Jesus," which is OK as long as you don't have to pronounce it.

(94) Fair Exchange Is No Robbery

The most exciting thing I've read in months was the *New York Times Magazine* story of the Caravaggio painting just discovered in Dublin. It seems that a Jesuit house had "The Taking of Christ" on the wall for 60 years. It was dark, much corrupted and stained by time. An art-expert found it, restored it, and authenticated it — and the picture is now on view at the National Gallery of Ireland. It was not offered for sale, but a Sotheby's representative said the painting would be "underpriced" at $36 million. This got me thinking.

The main features in my life would all be underpriced at $36 million. I wouldn't exchange Irene for that, or my kids (Molly or Nicholas or Rebecca). I wouldn't trade my friends (Charley, Larry, Jud, or Mike). Would I sell Boswell, my golden retriever, for $36 million? Forget it, buddy.

#94 – "FAIR EXCHANGE IS NO ROBBERY"

Sure I'd sell my house and car and computer for that, but not my personal treasures. The only question I have concerns Hodge, my white tomcat.

Would I sell Hodge for $36 million? I've only had him for two years. And since he's a cat, it's hard to say I *have* him. I feed him, and we kind of co-exist. But he's beautiful to be around, and last night when I was watching *Mystery*, he chose to jump up and sleep on my lap. It was a comfortable moment. I don't think I'd sell Hodge. I need him, somehow. I need his beauty, his fellowship, and his independent spirit. I need him more than I need $36 million.

(95) "Hawkins"

One of my favorite tabloid stories concerns the ghostly voice heard in a London cemetery. The *Weekly World News* told of Violet Joyce, who was sitting in a graveyard talking on a tape-recorder. (I forget why.) Later when she played back the tape, she heard a strange voice. Since she had been alone, it had to be a spirit talking. But the spirit didn't have much to say. It just repeated the word "Hawkins" over and over. Nobody has any idea what that means.

This brings up a central issue. If spirits from beyond wanted to communicate, what do they have to say to us? Woody Allen described a seance at which a man's brother brought him a message from the other world. He said wearing argyle stockings with a blue suit is a mistake.

(96) A Son of the Church

I am a loyal, lifetime Roman Catholic, and I think the Church is wrong on most issues relating to gender.

- I believe there should be women priests.
  What's so special about the male clergy
  we have now?
- We should discourage but permit divorce. Who
  can judge what goes on inside someone else's
  marriage?
- We should discourage, but tolerate abortion.
  Who says an early fetus is a human being?
- Artificial birth-control is fine with me. Sex
  organs are useful, but we should make
  important decisions with our brain.
- I want homosexuals to be regular communicants
  in the congregation. Why discriminate against
  people who are born different?

I believe all this and consider myself a good Catholic.

Holy Mother Church is like my wife. She's done great things for a long time, and she makes me rejoice about the world and other people and myself. The Church (like Irene) isn't perfect, but it's wonderful and I love it. I'm committed.

If I left the Church – with the Mass and the sacraments and the Creed, with Mary and St. Thomas and 2000 years of tradition – I'd be somebody else. I'm Catholic like I'm male, like I'm right-handed. I'll always be that way.

On these gender issues, the hierarchy will come around. I maintain that my church, the Holy Roman Catholic Church, is always right – within 300 years.

(97) Miss Manners Didn't Print My Letter

I wrote Miss Manners about a social issue which arose in Middleton, Wisconsin, last summer. I was enjoying civilized conversation in a lady's house when her

19-year-old daughter entered. To demonstrate how hot it was outside and how hard she'd been working, the dramatic young woman crawled up the stairs and into the living-room. She grunted "Hi" and lay there in apparent exhaustion.

I didn't know what to do, and Miss Manners never told me. I asked her, "Should a gentleman rise when a lady crawls into the room?"

(98) <u>Did Susan Call?</u>

For years every time I left the English office, I told my secretary, "If Susan calls, tell her I'm at home (or at Jud's or Bronco Billy's or wherever)." I've spent the last decade waiting for a phone-call from Susan Lucci.

This is the scenerio. Susan is sitting with her sister and feeling low. She says, "Helen, I'm frustrated. I know I have fame and fortune and millions of devoted fans and a fine husband and family and friends and jewels and a gorgeous wardrobe and all that New York City can offer — but it's not enough. There's too much pressure. I need to get away for a while — someplace where I can eat cheeseburgers and drink Red Dog beer and look out at the ocean. I've heard of a spot in Gulf Shores, Alabama, a place called the Pink Pony Pub. I'd like to relax on their porch and feel the sun and watch young people splashing in the Gulf of Mexico. I'd like to spend a few days down there, perhaps with a literate older man, someone I can talk to. Maybe an English professor."

Her sister will say, "I know just the man. My daughter is taking Freshman English at N.Y.U., and she's been reading this textbook called *The Language of Argument*. It's funny and insightful and provocative. My friend Patricia Rossi, who works at HarperCollins, knows the author. His name is McDonald, and she says he's charming and handsome and brimming with health. He's retired now, so he'll have time to enjoy the beach. I'm sure you can reach him, Susan. He lives in Mobile. Why not phone the English Department at the University of South Alabama? I'll bet they can put you through to him."

Yes, friend, I know this is a fantasy, and maybe it won't happen this week or next. *But it might*. So I make sure Mrs. Damico, the English Department secretary, always knows where I am. After all, I'm a Southern gentleman. I'd feel terrible if Susan Lucci called and couldn't get in touch with me.

(99) Matchmaking

Joyce Myer may be the best evangelist I hear on WMOB. But I have trouble following her too. The other day, she talked to a group of women and said they should pray for "the right mate." She said, "You need the mate God wants you to have. Not the mate you want to have. And not the mate the Devil wants you to have." I'm surprised she didn't mention "the mate your mother wants you to have."

Apparently there's a lot of matchmaking going on.

(100) Dying for a Cause

The main thing on television these days is the plight of the Chechens. The small republic of Chechnya challenged the Russian government and was bombed and invaded. The men died heroically.

For generations, the Chechens have died heroically. That's what they do. Through the communist decades, they defied the state and were cruelly repressed. Earlier, they defied the czars and were cruelly persecuted. Regularly, the tribes and clans attacked each other, and fought to the death. The Chechens are a fierce, bloody, and uncompromising people.

I told my friend Jud, "Chechen men seem to have no other goal than to die heroically. I don't understand it." As always, Jud's answer was provocative. He said, "Did you see their women?"

(101) A Charm for Every Occasion

If luck is running against you, maybe you haven't got what it takes. You need a talisman, a lucky-piece, a magic charm. Every tabloid advertises a dozen of them. Invariably, they promise money, love, health, success, and POWER!

Look them over. You can buy Lucky Lodestones, the Miracle Water Cross (said to contain Lourdes water), Rondo's Lucky Hand, the Pentacle of Mars, the Seal of Solomon, the Miraculous Sundial, Madame Zarina's Talisman, or ABRAXAS (a charm which invokes the power of the ancient Basilidians). You can also buy the LUCK-KEY, or a 12" x 24" replica of the Shroud of Turin. (The ad boasts it is small enough to fold in your pocket and take to the race-track.)

A few years ago, I sent for the LUCK-KEY. It only cost $4.00, and I thought it would be a nice conversation-piece on my key-ring. When it came, it was a strip of pink paper with a key drawn on it. (Sometimes you hear a voice in the air saying "Gotcha!")

Many people respond to these things. In a revealing story, the *National Enquirer* told of TV actress Joan Van Ark and her commitment to talismans and magic-tokens. It said that during one period of good fortune, she was carrying as many as 30 lucky-pieces, in her bra. What a charming woman she must have been.

(102) It's Not My Party

I have happy memories of teaching at Notre Dame, but not of the parties I went to. Routinely, year after year, Irene and I would be invited to parties, and when we got there, no one would talk to us. We'd make the usual overtures, but people weren't interested. It was a closed society. We'd stand by ourselves for a while; then we'd go home. Irene asked if I felt bad about these occasions, and I said, "No, it's not my party."

What I meant was that, when guests come to my house, I'll work hard to make them feel welcome and comfortable. I can't do anything about other people's indifference. So I don't worry about it. Also, I don't feel bad when I attend a pointless meeting or hear a dull sermon. It's not my party.

Indeed this is my attitude toward Heaven and Hell. I don't know about any afterlife. It may be glorious or grim or nothing. I don't worry about it. It's not my party.

(103) A Medical Breakthrough

I got new glasses last week. With the old lenses, everything looked fuzzy. When I came home with the new pair, I told Irene I was going to check out the TV to see how the glasses worked. I turned on an AMC movie. There on the screen was Jayne Mansfield doing an animated dance. From the kitchen, Irene asked how the glasses were, and I told her, "These are *wonderful* glasses. That Murray Glusman is a fine doctor."

(104) <u>Doing the Number</u>

Here's a lesson from an old magician. If I want to impress you with a magic effect, the main thing I'll avoid is simply doing the trick. That never works.

Suppose I have you pick a card from a deck and look at it. Immediately, I announce, "It's the seven of clubs." What's the result? You're not impressed. You'll say I forced a card on you, or it was a stacked deck or a marked deck, or I had a confederate helping me. It was "just a trick." So instead of doing the trick, a good magician will "do the number." He'll lay out a cloud of language to enhance the final revelation. (Stay with me, friend. There's a point to all this.)

If I were to do that trick, I'd begin with a serious, unhurried prologue. I'd say, "OK, I'll try this if you want me to, but you have to remember that sometimes it doesn't work. Although sometimes it does. I've always had a gift for knowing things, for seeing things. Grandma McCredden used to say I had second-sight. When I was in grade-school, she'd always send me to find lost objects. Often I could. Over the years, I've had some success doing mental effects, but I sure don't know how I do them.

"To begin with, I want you to do everything you can to keep me from fooling you. (Remember this is either a psychic insight or it's a card-trick.) Shuffle the deck carefully. Get a different deck if you want to. When I offer the cards, don't choose any one it looks like I'm forcing on you. When you take a card, don't let me or anyone else see it. But you have to look at it. Stare at it hard. Let the figure on the front almost burn itself in your brain. When I identify things, I'm never sure if I'm seeing the thing itself or if I'm reading someone's mind. I just don't know.

#64 - "ST. DANIEL OF MOBILE"

And, as I said, sometimes I can't identify anything. I tried this effect at the Knights of Columbus last month, and it was a disaster. All right, I'm ready if you are. Pick a card."

You'll choose one, and I'll know instantly (through any of a dozen systems) that it is the seven of clubs. So I say — *nothing*. I stare at my feet for 30 seconds (that's a long time in this context), then I say, "Did you look at the card carefully? I'm not getting anything." Another 30 seconds go by. Then I mutter, "This isn't working." But I'm game. I say, "Let's give it one last try. You don't have to look at your card again, but I ask you to really, really concentrate on it. OK, you're doing that? Fine." After 15 seconds, I say, "Let's give it up." I apologize, "All I'm getting is that your card is not an ace or a face-card. There are a fair number of spots on it. If I had to guess, I'd say it's black." Another 15-second pause, then I stammer out the truth, "I think — I think it's a spade — NO, no, it's — it's a club. It's either — either the six — or it could be the seven — of clubs. It's coming into focus now. Yeah, that's what it looks like. Tell me, Paul [I always insert a name here], is your card the seven of clubs?"

That's what's called "doing the number."

I mention this because it occurs to me that the best parts of our lives involve preliminaries, doing a number. Plays have prologues, music has preludes, football games have pep-rallies, Las Vegas headliners have opening-acts. We spend months on wedding preparations. At church, we have Baptism and the Last Rites. In family life, we have hors d'oeuvres, and varieties of foreplay, and presents wrapped under the Christmas tree. All these, of course, are part of the forthcoming event. They make it richer and more meaningful.

I'm reminded that in June 1955, I gave Irene a gold wedding-band. Engraved inside it was a line from *The Tempest*. It celebrated the preceding years: our graduate work at the University of Wisconsin, the coffee-conversations after Mass, some wonderful friends, and our months of courtship. My wife has worn the ring for 40 years now, and the message is as relevant as ever. It says, "What's past is prologue."

(105) Dying for a Heineken

In my refrigerator, I keep a few bottles of Heineken and a dozen cans of Budweiser. The cans are for guests; the bottles are for me. It's a matter of life and death.

Whenever I wonder which beer to have, I think about mortality. I could get shot tonight, or have that coronary. I know death is inevitable, and it doesn't bother me. The world will go on. My kids will inherit my stuff. My wife will remarry. I can't do anything about that. But I'd hate to die knowing someone else will drink that great beer I *could* have had. So at the moment of truth, I always grab a Heineken.

Who says you can't take it with you?

(106) Where Will It All End?

Last week at K&B, I saw the latest issue of the *Sun*. The headline read:

"FACTS ABOUT THE END OF THE WORLD
REVEALED — THE DATE AND THE PLACE"

That's got me worried.

It never dawned on me the end of the world would be localized, that it could happen in a particular place. God, it might be anywhere! I imagine calling my friend Harvey in San Diego. I'll ask, "How are things going with you?" And he'll say, "Dan, it's horrible. It's the end of the world out here. Jordine and I can't – " I hate to think about that.

I went back to K&B to buy the tabloid so I'd have exact information, but it was sold out. Now I may never know where the end of the world will occur. I should have bought the *Sun* when I had a chance.

(107) The Ultimate Foreign Language

Last Saturday, Gregory and Natalya came to lunch, along with Svetlana, Irene's language teacher. It was time to talk Russian.

I told them not to mind me. I would sit there and enjoy the conversation. And I did. I especially enjoyed watching Svetlana, a charmer who speaks perfect English, take great pleasure in talking her native tongue. Everyone had a good time, but she was glowing.

After lunch, I said, "It must be a joy to talk Russian after all these years in America." She said, "Dan, no matter how well you know a foreign language, it's still foreign. There are presuppositions that go with one's native language."

"I know that," I said. "I've been talking to women for years. I'm very gifted; I speak gender flawlessly. But when I'm with men, I can relax and just talk." Svetlana called me a chauvinist, and we both laughed. But what I said is true.

Gender is a foreign language.

(108) Handling the Rejection Letter

Question: What do you do when you send a piece off to be published, and the editor abuses it? You don't receive the usual card saying "We regret this does not meet our current needs." You get a nasty letter. I know how to deal with this.

Last month I got back a 6-page essay from a national journal. (Let's call it *Mature Christian Athlete*.) The editor included a 400-word rejection-letter. He said my argument was wrong-headed; the logic was shaky; the humor was forced; and my language was sexist. He said the article was a type his magazine used to publish, but doesn't any more. He wrote, "We haven't printed this kind of thing since I've been here, and we won't as long as I'm the editor." The gentleman was having a bad day.

I handled the situation with great skill. I put my essay and his rejection-letter in a manila envelope and mailed them back to him. My cover-note said, "I hate to press you. But I'm going to need a firm answer on this."

(109) The Mark of the Intellectual

I am always proud of my son Nicholas. But rarely more than the day I went to Sun-Ray, a local grocery where he had a high-school job as stock-boy. The sign over the counter advertised "10^3 ISLAND DRESSING." My heart leaped up. I knew Nick's handiwork.

(110) Calling from the Mall

When I go to Bel Air Mall, I like to sit at a table in front of Barnie's and drink their mocha-java coffee. I find lots of adventure there.

From my chair, I command a rich view. I can see people entering and exiting the Mall and walking the long corridor in front of me. Today I watched a 50-year-old man in a white shirt. I saw him come around the corner by Parisian and walk 100 yards to the exit. *He was talking on a cordless phone the whole time.* I couldn't hear what he said, but twice he stopped and made animated gestures. Something was going on. I wondered. Was he saying "Phone the Shell station. They'll come pick it up"? Or "I know that, Honey. Apologize to your mother for me."? It occurred to me he might also be a charlatan talking into a dead telephone.

And that's my new fantasy. I want to sit for two hours in front of Barnie's talking into a phone. When people are around to listen, I'll deliver memorable lines. I'll say:

> "We can make a fortune on this, Harry. When TMS gets to 74, sell. Sell all we have."
> > [or]
> "Believe me, Honey, Monica means nothing to me."
> > [or, in frustration]
> "I didn't say 'paralysis'; I said 'dialysis'."

There's no limit to my scope here. When the moment and the audience is right, I can play a Mafia role. Listeners will hear me whisper:

> "The shipment is coming in on Wednesday. It's on a Danish freighter called *Rouselle*. That's 'Rouselle' with an 'R'."
> > [Or, in a climactic moment]
> "Listen. Paulie had his chance to pay up and he didn't. Send Vito around to talk to him."

Things don't have to get this dramatic. It occurs
to me my most provocative lines could be responses to
some imaginary caller. I can pause and nod and say
"Uh-hunh" a lot. I can interject "Don't you believe it!"
or "She said there were 14 of them" or "You spell it
M-O-G-B-U-E? OK, I've got that down." I'll give my
audience a lot to think about. In a favorite moment, I
will purr, "Sweetheart, of course I'm concerned. Tell
me the whole story." Then I'll put my phone on the
table and walk into Barnie's for another cup of coffee.
I'll have a lot of fun with that phone.

The man I saw in the Mall today enriched my
life. Maybe I can enrich somebody else's. How are
you going to spend your retirement?

(111) A Brief Survey

As I stood in the check-out line at K&B waiting to pay
for my 12-pack of Red Dog, I saw a headline on the
latest issue of *Reader's Digest*. It said: "WHAT MEN
DON'T UNDERSTAND ABOUT WOMAN." Immediately I
picked up the magazine and counted. It had 208 pages.
"Well," I thought, "they're probably just touching on
some of the major areas."

(112) The Holy Trinity

What does the Christian doctrine of the Trinity mean?
I'm glad you asked me that. I have the feeling
nobody else can tell you.

If there's a God, I don't know what He's like. But
the idea of a Trinity helps. The doctrine says that God
exists as three persons: the Father, the Son, and the
Holy Spirit — *and the three are one*. That's tricky.

I've heard priests try to compare this to a three-
leaf clover, but that doesn't work. Each part of the

clover is only a part.   According to the doctrine, God the Father isn't just part of God. He's the whole thing. And so is the Son, and so is the Holy Spirit. A clover is different. I've heard teachers use the metaphor of water, which exists as solid and liquid and gas. But this doesn't work either. The ice is not the steam, and the fluid isn't the ice. Each part of the Trinity has to be all of it. Ice-water-steam is different.

What's the answer?   The answer is the Trinity doesn't make sense. And that's how it manifests God. It says God is beyond human reason. He's not like you and me. He's not George Burns or Mother Teresa or Julius Caesar or Clark Kent. He exits on another wave-length. He's something else.

I go to church every Sunday. Can I have a personal relationship with a being I don't understand? Sure I can. This morning I attended a Spanish Mass and rejoiced in the beautiful and affectionate people, their dark-eyed children, their bright colors, their syncopated music, and their intense faith. I loved them; they are my brothers and sisters in Christ. But I didn't understand a word they said. Loving God isn't that much different, I think. It might not be different at all.

(113) Journalistic Perfection

There are moments when you have to grab the beauty and savor it. Today at Barnes & Noble, I saw the latest issue of *Esquire*. The scarlet headline blared, "MAILER ON MADONNA." God, how perfect! In one swell foop, I can ignore *Esquire*; I don't have to read Mailer; I won't hear about Madonna; and I save $2.50. Wow! I only wish the magazine cost $100 and you had to go to California to buy it.

#110 - "CALLING FROM THE MALL"

(114) Alzheimer's and Pi

Five years ago, my blood-pressure was in the 180/110 range, and I was having problems. My head was loggy; I wasn't quick; I couldn't remember things. Dr. Remington looked me over and suggested, among other possibilities, that I might be getting Alzheimer's Disease. I responded to this typically: I got angry at my doctor. I thought, "I'll show that sawbones," and went home and memorized pi to 528 places. (Pi, you remember, is the ratio of a circle's diameter to its circumference. It's a never-ending decimal.)

Well, the health problem is gone now. My blood-pressure is down. (I take a pill every day, and I don't eat anything good.) But I can still read off pi to 200 places, and I'm likely to. When I hear someone discussing memory or mathematics or the area of a circle (they might wonder if a 12-inch pizza is larger than two 6-inch pizzas) — I may announce "I know about that. I can recite pi to 200 places." And I begin, "3.14159265358979323846264338327950288419-796939937510 ..."

As you can imagine, not everyone is thrilled to hear me parrot my numbers. I don't get invited to parties much anymore.

(115) Bad News, Bad News, and Bad News

Two days ago, the *Mobile Press Register* had articles insisting that dogs should not attend Mardi Gras parades. Yesterday, it had a long section in which young couples told why they've chosen not to have children. Today, the hot story concerns a New Jersey husband who is suing his wife for divorce claiming she committed adultery on the Internet.

When the current is running against my major
values (dogs, babies, full-contact sex), I begin to worry.
I'm not going to read tomorrow's paper. I know
there'll be an article saying beer causes cancer.

(116) The Wisconsin Muse

I remember in 1945 (the year I graduated from Black
River Falls High School) there was a contest to name
Arnie Johnson's new barber-shop. First prize was $25,
and second prize was $10. The second prize went to
"Black River Barber Shop." (We didn't have salons or
styling-centers back then.) The grand-prize winner was
"Johnson's Barber Shop."

I tell you this in case you wonder where I got
my creative insights.

(117) All Right, Louie, Drop That Newspaper

Wives are wonderful people and they say lots of things
worth listening to, but a man needs time off. At the
last meeting of the Gulf Coast Humanities Consortium,
one member (I'll call him Jason) told how he handles
the problem.

"The first step," Jason said, "is the newspaper.
When Amy is rambling on about her boss and her
mother and Jessica and money and the car and all the
jobs I should be doing around the house, I sit there
reading the sports-page. (The Braves have won seven
in a row!) Pretty soon, she'll ask 'Are you listening to
me?' This is my moment. I lower the paper, turn my
chair five degrees toward her, and say 'Of course, I'm
listening. Please continue.' Then she'll rattle on, and I
go back to reading the paper. (I didn't lower it very
far.) Now I wait to hear some word spoken with
emphasis. I repeat it in the form of a question.

('Fifteen?' I'll ask. 'Yes, fifteen,' she'll answer. 'Can you believe that?') And always I wait for a pause. This means she's taking a breath, or maybe she expects a response. I used to say 'Unhunnh' and 'Oh yes,' but I'm getting a better result with 'And then what happened?' All this works great. Amy loves it. She thinks we're having a family discussion."

OK, men, you've heard the agenda: 1) lower the newspaper, 2) reposition your chair, 3) echo key words, and 4) say "Then what happened?" This sequence should work for you. Jason says his love-life has improved considerably since he mastered the art of conversation.

(118) A Cure for Insomnia II

Last month, I read about a new movie, *The Madness of King George*. It was originally titled *The Madness of George III*, but producers feared people would think it a follow-up picture, like *Godfather II* or *Halloween III*. Since reading this, I've had no trouble falling asleep. I lie in bed and think of sequels.

I imagine theater marquees offering Neil Simon's *Chapter II*, Billy Wilder's *One, Two III*, and Sherlock Holmes in *The Sign Of IV*. I think of wonderfully successful series climaxing in *Oceans XI*, *Stalag XVII*, and (incredibly) *Route LXVI* and *PT CIX*. Tonight you can add titles to this list.

Be warned. As you near sleep, you'll begin to lose concentration. You'll think of Lee Marvin in *The Big Red I* and *The Dirty XII*. You'll remember Marilyn Monroe in *The Year Itch VII*. Hopefully, you'll drop off before you come to *And Then There Were 0* and *The Postman Always Rings II*.

Sweet dreams.

(119) God's Name

A long-running tabloid ad speaks to people who feel their prayers haven't been answered. It counsels civility. You get better results when you call people by name, it says. Therefore, when you want God's help, you should address him by his name. If you write to a Texas church, they will tell you God's name.

I wrote in. God's name is Yahweh.

(120) It's Not Easy Being a Liberal

Yesterday a Pensacola jury voted to execute a 22-year-old boy. I have mixed feelings about it.

As a knee-jerk liberal, I oppose the death-penalty. I think it is cruel and inhuman. I think it pairs me with the morals of the killers being executed. The Pensacola defendant is my brother in Christ. Maybe something could be done to help him. I know all this.

On the other hand, he was one of three men who broke into the home of a 38-year-old banker. They shot him in the back of the head, then brutalized and raped his wife. It's hard to find a scenario which justifies this.

So the young man is going to live in a cage for four or five years, enduring the savagery and dehumanization of prison life. Then he will be strapped in a chair and microwaved. That's a sad future. I wish I felt worse about it."

(121) The Five Best Things

When you're in your 60s, you can look back and make judgments. Last month at a lounge in Bangor, Wales, I sat with six Elderhostlers and drank Heineken beer. We speculated about the Five Best Things in Life. When I gave my list, I said I couldn't do it in 1-5 order. That would distort things.

For me, the No. 1 best thing is babies. No. 2 is golden retrievers. Nos. 3-9 are blank, because nothing else is nearly as good as those first two. Then comes a tie for Nos. 10/11: beer and coffee. (I quoted the sweat-shirt motto: "If it weren't for caffeine, I wouldn't have any personality at all.") And Nos. 12-27 are blank. At No. 28, in a kind of random choice, I named the Macintosh computer.

My friends had similar lists. (We all put babies as No. 1.) They mentioned true love, the Mass, cats, Jack Benny, Lilacs, *Don Giovanni*, Ireland, running-shoes, etc. One lady made a case for Chinese food. Her husband said he couldn't conceive of a best-list that didn't include the 1947 Yankees. There were no big arguments. We agreed that life has a lot to offer and we've enjoyed our 60-plus years.

Then we ordered another Heineken.

(122) <u>Godzilla The Destroyer</u>

How can you resist the *Weekly World News* headline: "GODZILLA WRECKED MY MARRIAGE"?

The story concerns an Illinois couple, Jana and Leon Giurek, who (after a lush dinner and two bottles of champagne) drove to a motel to spend their wedding-night. While she was in the bathroom making herself perfect, Leon — with the sensitivity that has made men a legend — switched on the television. To his joy, he found a Godzilla movie. And not just any Godzilla movie, it was *Godzilla Meets the Smog Monster*. When Jana came out, he suggested they order a pot of coffee and stay up and watch the film. She refused. He got angry and finally stomped out. She is now suing him for divorce on grounds of cruelty.

As my friend Jerry Wilkerson used to say, "Woman, who knows what they will do?"

(123) Hey, Look at What Never Happened!

I love it when tabloids celebrate events which they admit never happened. The *Weekly World News* published an exposé: "Jane Fonda Denies Having Fling with Gorbachev." Later it headlined: "Vanna Not Pregnant!" One issue of the *National Examiner* had two sensational stories. One explained why Natalie Wood did not have an affair with Elvis. The other told why she didn't have an affair with James Dean.

This is encouraging journalism. I fantasize there will someday be a definitive analysis of the Dan McDonald / Susan Lucci relationship.

(124) Credit Where Credit Is Due

Last week down at Gulf State Lodge, I did an Elderhostel program on Gilbert and Sullivan. It went great. We played the songs from *Trial by Jury*, *H. M. S. Pinafore*, and *The Mikado*. Classroom-volunteers read the acting-parts; I explained things; and everyone followed along with a script. The music was rollicking (Koko sings "The Flowers That Bloom in the Spring, Tra La"). The lines were funny. (Katisha boasts "I have a left shoulder-blade that is a miracle of loveliness.") And everyone laughed and sang along.

When the course was finished, a lady came up and said, "Doctor, I loved this class. You did such a wonderful job." I wasn't sure how to answer her. I knew I'd done an entertaining program, but I was hugely aided by W. S. Gilbert's dialogue, by Sir Arthur Sullivan's music, by Martin Green's singing, and by the

D'oyly Carte Opera Company. Should I take credit for
all that?

Quickly, I thought back. I thought of all the times
I've been blamed for things I didn't do. I remembered
cars honking at me because traffic was backed up. I
recalled students blaming me for policies the English
Department had established. And I heard Irene's voice
blaming me for things the kids did, or the computer
did, or God did. Why shouldn't I get credit for some
good things?

So when the lady praised me for the Gilbert and
Sullivan class, I answered modestly. "Thank you," I
said. "I try to do a good job."

(125) Consortium Adventures

The Gulf Coast Humanities Consortium is the best thing
to happen to me since Rebecca. The Consortium can be
viewed in two ways. Either it is a scholarly
organization containing 60 members, which meets every
month or so to discuss ideas — or it is five guys who
drive to the Pink Pony Pub in Gulf Shores to drink
Rolling Rock, eat cheeseburgers, look at the girls, and
argue about things. Either view is defensible.

Active members are two English professors, a
priest, a communications-consultant, and a TV anchor-
man. Other members are a lot of people who agreed
we could use their names. They include a college
president, a judge, a district-attorney, a famous outdoor
author, a masseuse, an airline executive, lots of
professors, some newspaper reporters, and one reporter
from the *National Enquirer*. If these people could get
to our meetings, we'd love to see them. But they
never come. (Each meeting begins with toasts to
absent members.)

#17 - "HOOTERS AND GOOD VALUES"

We are not a typical academic organization. These are pretty dull. I remember flying to a big city, staying at a hotel, and wearing my blue suit. Either I didn't go to the scholarly sessions, or I did go and didn't listen, or I went and listened, and the papers were pointless or incomprehensible. There was no discussion of issues. At Consortium meetings, someone reads a paper and it had better be good. The speaker can be challenged at any time. Cries of "Nonsense!" and "Oh, come off it!" are not uncommon. Presentations are routinely interrupted by someone calling out "Innkeeper" or "Isn't it nice to see young people enjoying the beach." Regularly we affirm togetherness and the good life.

We reject any charge that the Consortium is not politically correct. We remind critics that, among our very earliest members, we admitted a Protestant. Women are welcome as members, but they must fulfill two conditions: 1) They must be cute, and 2) they must live 200 miles from Mobile.

We have not had a meeting for awhile, because members are occupied with new babies. But we're due. At the next program (which may be at the Grand Hotel), Father David will speak on Robert Bolt's *The Mission*.

(126) Pot Evidence

I write books on persuasion, and I love it when I see conclusive proof. That is evidence no one can refute, evidence which ends the argument. I think of this because I just saw a *Parade* article asking whether marijuana is physically harmful to the smoker.

We settled this question in my Argument class ten years ago. After we read an essay defending marijuana, Wendy — a pretty blonde — said she could give us absolute proof that pot-smoking is physically dangerous. Then she showed us a scar. She had burned her thumb at a fraternity party the night before.

I guess that settles that.

(127) The Wrong Name

I left there 50 years ago, but my commitment to my home-town in Wisconsin has never diminished. I showed this again last night.

My daughter Rebecca phoned from Texas where she manages a La Madeleine restaurant. She said she'd been doing some catering for a strange woman. This was a lady who had moved to Austin because her name is Austin. She didn't particularly like the town, but she felt it was where she had to live.

"That's a tough break," I said. "If her name was Black River Falls, she'd have it made."

(128) Divine Editing

If you think English-teacher editing isn't important, listen to this.

A recent story in the *Weekly World News* tells of Jane Palzere, a Connecticut woman who has just published the letters of Jesus. She produced them by automatic writing, with Jesus controlling her hand. In the letters, he discusses abortion, suicide, marijuana, the energy crisis, bad habits, and UFOs.

The first message she received began, "You are going to be the channel for the writing of a book." Then came the words "Love Jesus." The second message told her she should have put a comma after "love." "Jesus" was a signature.

(129) <u>Close Enough</u>

Just when you think there's nothing on television but
sex, violence, and banal talk, you stumble on a
treasure. This morning, I flipped on the tube and sat
back to eat my Wheaties. I was thrilled by what I
heard.

I don't know what the program was. The first
scene showed a bosomy blonde in a revealing gown,
complaining to a friend. Apparently it's her wedding-
day and her husband is away. She says, "Wherever Jim
is, I know he's enjoying himself, having the time of his
life." She is wrong. In the next scene, we see Jim, a
muscled young man, strung up from a ceiling. He is
about to be tortured. (So far, it was standard TV
fare.)

As I crossed the room to turn off the set, I
heard arresting dialogue. A bearded older man – the
evil torturer – reminds Jim of some past offense and
says, "My object all sublime is to make the punishment
fit the crime." I stopped dead. I'd heard a literary
allusion. The torturer adds, "That's from Dostoevsky."
Jim, hanging in chains, can endure torture but not
misquotation. He grunts, "That's from Gilbert and
Sullivan." And the villain wins the day with his
memorable response. He says, "Close enough."

When I clicked off the TV, the man was reaching
for some torture device. I didn't need to see more.
But I am still caught by that sequence: "Dostoevsky....
Gilbert and Sullivan.... Close enough." I'm thrilled by
the literature of indiscrimination.

I remember rich examples. Back in the 40s,
there was a comic-strip called *The Nut Brothers*. In
one sequence, Ches is a cook watching his brother Wal
eat dinner. He boasts, "My two best dishes are corn-

beef hash and custard-pie." And Wal asks, "Which is this?" My favorite example came to me 20 years ago in a Three Dog Night lyric. The singer finds consolation in the line "I ain't never been to Spain, but I been to Oklahoma." If you're looking for indiscrimination, friend, you'll never do better than that.

(130) Play It Again, Sam

For me, the ultimate love-song will always be Leroy Anderson's "Blue Tango." In my young days, I heard that beat and fell in complete, total, final, and everlasting love — at least twice. I also fell in love hearing "Deep Purple," "Stardust," "Blueberry Hill," and "I Wonder Who's Kissing Her Now."

I think of this because I just heard "Blue Tango" on my car-radio and remembered Patricia. (God bless her.) Also, last week I phoned the University's English Department and was put on hold. When the secretary came back on the line, she apologized for the delay. "Forget it, Kathy," I said. "Women have been putting me on hold since 1942."

(131) My True Name

An ad in the *Astrology and Psychic News* carried the provocative headline: "DO YOU HAVE THE RIGHT NAME?"

It began, "Millions of people are misnamed at birth, causing them problems and unhappiness throughout their lives." They feel "lethargic, sad, and lacking in energy." The solution is simple: Send $16.50 to Krishna Ram-Davi. He will meditate on your behalf and tell you your true first name. The ad said you don't have to change your present name; just knowing your true name will bring wonderful benefits.

There may be something to this. When I retired from teaching, the University gave me an office out at its Brookley campus. When I got there, I found a plastic name-plate on my door. It said "BIG DAN." Inside on my desk was another name-plate: "Dr. Daniel L. McDonald." Immediately I threw away the second plate. I had found my true name. I am Big Dan, and I feel great about it.

(132) My Movie Schedule

In my retirement, I enjoy a regular schedule of moviegoing. I don't go to pictures during the year. I wait until spring to see which film wins the Academy Award as "Movie of the Year." Then I don't go to that either.

(133) The Existential Moment

Every so often in a person's life, there comes an existential moment — a time when you say, "Here I am in a strange universe" and ask "What's it all about, Alfie?" I had such a moment 25 years ago.

I was home alone one afternoon. (Irene and the kids were off at some grade-school function.) I was awakened from a nap by the ringing telephone. Half-asleep, I staggered out to the family-room and grunted, "Hello." It was 10-year-old Philip Molyneux who wanted to speak to Nick. I said, "He isn't here." Phillip said nothing. I said, "Nick will be back around 4:00." Phillip said nothing. I asked if he would like to leave a message. Phillip said, "Just a minute. I'll get a pencil," and left the phone.

There I stood half-asleep, waiting for Phillip, and trying to understand my role in the universe.

#134 - "MCDONALD'S LAW"

(134) McDonald's Law

We all know Murphy's Law ("Anything that can go wrong, will"); some of us know Herblock's Law ("If it's any good, they'll stop making it"); and CBS is now giving us *Burke's Law*. I'm here with McDonald's Law. Or laws — there are seven of them. They're not all original, but who cares? I got them somewhere, and I live by them.

1) There *is* a free lunch. (I eat it all the time.)
2) If you don't say it, you won't have to explain it.
3) There are no calories out of town. (In particular, there are no calories when you're in an airplane flying over water.)
4) What's sauce for the goose is sauce for the duck.
5) Women are wonderful when they're serving Hooterburgers or when they're your daughter on the long-distance phone.
6) If you tell the truth, you don't have to remember what you said.
7) Hey, it's beer time!

Are these claims true? I have no idea. They work for me.

(135) Encompassing Faith

On his radio show, "The Truck Driver's Special," evangelist Maes Jackson made a sweeping statement of scriptural faith. He said, "I believe every chapter in this Bible, every verse, every word." Then he added, "I even believe the outside."

Think about that if you have trouble getting to sleep tonight.

(136) EEOC, Get a Life

As I write this, the Equal Employment Opportunity Commission is going after Hooters. They want 40 percent of their servers and bartenders to be male. They want $23,000,000 set aside to compensate frustrated men who tried to get jobs at Hooters and were rejected for being the wrong gender. That's sexism, they claim, and it's illegal. This is crazy thinking, of course, but I kind of like it. Irene and I stand to make a bundle.

We're going to sue the Dallas Cowboys. Irene is distressed hat the team hasn't hired her (or any other women) to play football. They even boast of this, calling themselves "CowBOYS." I will complain that the Dallas Cheerleaders have excluded me. That's sexism, big time. Also we'll observe that the team has no players of my weight (160 pounds), and the Cheerleaders have no women of Irene's age (early 60s). That's sizism and ageism — and both are illegal. We'll even mention that Irene is Russian. Was it political, cold-war discrimination that kept her off Jerry Jones' payroll?

If Jones can give all that money to Dejon Sanders, he can come up with a few million to compensate Irene and me. We've got a helluva case. I've written the EEOC, and we're talking to our lawyer in the morning.

(137) And Now the Hard Question

My brother-in-law is a chef who occasionally gives lectures on cooking. John says the hardest question he ever received came from a 70-year-old woman in Keuka Park, New York. She asked, "What is the difference between a fresh turkey and a frozen turkey?" After some stammering, he explained that one was frozen and the other wasn't This seemed to satisfy her.

I was reminded of this incident yesterday when I was at P&A's Hair Salon. I heard a stylist talking to the lady in her chair. She asked, "But what do *you* mean by one inch?"

(138) Psychometry for Beginners

It's easy to do psychic readings. I proved this every quarter in my Argument class.

I had students give me articles they owned. Then I held the objects and felt their psychic vibrations. (Either that or I lied.) From these, I told class-members hidden truths about themselves. I said:

- You don't look it, but you have a secret
    sorrow that disturbs you deeply.
- Your life is chaotic right now. You need
    to get organized.
- You're OK now, but you've come through
    a period of emotional turmoil. (Don't worry.
    You made the right decisions.)
- You have a distressing secret, and you'd
    feel terrible if anyone knew. (Don't worry.
    I'm not going to tell.)
- You are hanging on to some thing (or some
    person) you know you should let go of.
- I see a door. You're about to enter a new
    phase in your life. Think carefully.
    This is a crucial time.

You get the idea. Name me somebody these readings *don't* fit. I just say them with heavy seriousness while holding a personal object. People are impressed by this nonsense. If you want to hear more, call a 900-number psychic some night.

At least I didn't charge $5.00 a minute.

(139) Communicating on Bourbon Street

When I taught at Southern Illinois University, one of my colleagues was Miss Burns, a lady in her 50s who was a fine English teacher, though perhaps a bit precise. She told us of Penny Jenkins, a freshman she had taught, who wasn't keen and wasn't interested in learning to write. She dropped out of school in the first quarter.

Months later, Miss Burns took a vacation trip to New Orleans and, as part of the tour, she visited some Bourbon Street nightspots. At one, she saw Penny Jenkins. Penny was wearing very little and dancing on the bar to the beat of "Sweet Georgia Brown." Ever the English teacher, Miss Burns was able to praise her student. "Penny had improved," she said. "She had finally mastered unity, coherence, and emphasis."

(140) Spell-checker Choices

The spell-check on my Macintosh is wonderful. It keeps asking me if I really want to write "interminible" and "kdog." Wouldn't I prefer "interminable" and "dog"? I'm not a confident speller, so I appreciate the help.

The fun comes when I write a proper name and the program suggests alternatives. Yesterday, I wrote about my friend "Jud" and was told I could substitute "mud" or "Judas." (Jud would love this.) When I wrote "Goya," I was offered "gay" and "gooey." In recent essays, I referred to Mike "Hanna," "No-Doz," "Barnie's" coffee, and Oscar "Wilde." My computer suggested the possibility of "Hawaiian," "nudes," "barrenness," and "wallowed." When I mentioned my dog "Boswell," I was offered "bacilli." Instead of Jack "Palance," the machine suggested "polonaise."

I'm an existentialist, so I love choices. Some of these, however, could tempt a man into excesses.

(141) The New Garbage Can

Three weeks ago, Irene and I drove to Wal-Mart and bought a new garbage-can. It's a beauty. It's large and green and has wheels and a snap-on top. As of today, we haven't put anything in it.

For years we had a regular garbage-can and an old one we used to carry leaves. When the main can was full, we put refuse in the other one. The old can had no top, the bottom had several holes, and the sides were splitting. Finally when we put it out on the curb, a kindly trash-man didn't just empty it; he carried it away. So we went out to buy another can.

The green can is fresh and new. It sits in our carport and shines in the sun. Irene thinks we shouldn't use it just for everyday. We have an ordinary can for that. The new one should be saved for special occasions. So, last night, I jammed two plastic garbage-bags and a big pile of newspaper in the old can so I wouldn't have to soil the new one. It's possible we won't use the new garbage-can until Christmas. If then.

I'm worried. This makes a kind of sense to me.

(142) Sexual Harassment

The University of South Alabama just adopted a "revised sexual harassment policy." I wrote Dean Allen and told him I'm glad I've retired from teaching. I'm a healthy 67-year-old man, and if I were back in the classroom, I'm capable of sexual harassment. But I'm not sure I'm up to revised sexual harassment. Where are the snows of yesteryear?

(143) The Null Set

There aren't many places where glaucoma and public-speaking go together. I found one last year when Dr. Rich, my ophthalmologist, invited me to address a class of medical assistants. My subject: "The Early Symptoms of Glaucoma."

I didn't see the problem with this until I started preparing my talk. The problem: There are *no* early symptoms of glaucoma. So when I spoke to the group, I took 15 seconds. I said, "I never felt any symptoms. I only knew I had glaucoma when I went in for a routine checkup and my doctor said I had it." Dr. Rich agreed. Pointing to me, he said, "This kind just comes in off the street."

There were other patients there who had kinds of glaucoma which have symptoms. So the evening was instructive.

Later I told Dr. Rich I was scheduling him to speak to the Gulf Coast Humanities Consortium. He had a choice of topics. He could discuss "The Healing Waters of Casablanca" or "Republican Plans to Aid the Homeless" or "Scholar-Athletes at Texas A&M." I asked that he limit his talk to 10 minutes.

(144) Golf Priorities

At the Elderhostel in Gulf Shores last week, I taught Gilbert and Sullivan operettas, and Terry Cline taught Storytelling. The third feature of the program was Golf. Most participants came for the golf.

For many of these people, golf is a way of life. I knew this, but I never saw it so clearly as when I overheard a breakfast conversation. The speakers were handsome Elderhostel ladies:

FIRST LADY: "What is your handicap?"
SECOND LADY: "Oh, I don't play golf."
FIRST LADY: "What do you do?"

(145) Remembering the Memorare

Last month, Irene and I attended Sunday Mass in Dalkeith, Scotland. At the end, the congregation began to pray the Memorare. They said: "Remember, O most gracious Virgin Mary, that never was it known that anyone who fled to your protection, implored your help..." The words seemed familiar and, little by little, whispering, I started to pray along: "... or sought your intercession, was left unaided. Inspired by this confidence, I fly unto you, O Virgin of virgins, my Mother...." Now I was reciting aloud; I *knew* this prayer. We finished up: "To you I come, before you I stand, sinful and sorrowful. O Mother of the Word Incarnate, despise not my petitions, but in your mercy hear and answer me. Amen."

After Mass, Irene said she didn't know the prayer, and she was surprised that I did. I said, "Sister Cordis taught it to me in the sixth grade at Black River Falls." It was amazing. I had learned the Memorare 55 years before, and I knew I hadn't heard it in 50 years. Yet, on cue, I remembered it and prayed it.

There are several messages here: That elementary teachers shape lives. That we never outgrow our grade-school selves. That the human brain is an incredible thing. (How were those words stored for 50 years?) The Memorare may have been an important

#72 – "SALT-FREE LIVING"

prayer to me at one time, I don't know. It's an important prayer now.

(146) Ask Serena

Every issue of the *Weekly World News* has a letters-to-the-expert column called "Ask Serena." The author is Serena Sabak, and in case you didn't notice the photograph, she's identified as "America's Sexiest Psychic." Her answers are traditional, but the questions are wonderfully provocative. Here are a few of them:

- Why is my 3-year-old boy speaking Latin?
- What happened to the silver dollar my uncle gave me in 1940?
- Should I let my boyfriend saw me in half?
- Was I a World War 2 flying ace in a past life?
- Which should I marry, Jonathan or Charley?

These questions had rich answers, of course, many of them involving spirit possession.

You'll be pleased to hear that Serena advised the girl not to let her boyfriend saw her in half. (He was an amateur magician.) And she told the other girl not to marry either Jonathan or Charley. She should marry Tim.

(147) Nostalgia. Anyone?

I was born in the 1920s and grew up in a different world. In Black River Falls, Wisconsin, we enjoyed real Coke, unfiltered Lucky Strikes, Blatz beer, Maxwell House coffee, Heinz catsup, Armour hot-dogs, bottled milk with the cream on top, and unprotected sex. Today as I walk through Delchamps, I see Diet Pepsi, Carlton cigarettes, Lite beer, Sanka coffee, Healthy Choice ketchup, Hormel 97% Fat-Free Franks, and homogenized and skim milk. Next door at Harco, there's a huge display of condoms and spermicides.

Are things better in the 90s? Maybe. But it sure seems plastic to me.

(148) Blindness Isn't So Bad

OK, I'm older now and I've lost a fair amount of eyesight. There are compensations for that.

My wife and I were at the university gym last Monday, and I was sitting at a rowing-machine when I dropped my towel. Turning I said, "Honey, will you pick that up for me?" The girl next to me, who I thought was my wife, said, "Sure thing" and handed it over. Irene saw this. She saw I had confused her with a girl who is 20 pounds lighter than she is, and 40 years younger. She wasn't offended. She was very nice to me all that day.

Another compensation is the $43,000 I saved last month. I had planned to buy an Olds Cutlass this fall, but my vision got bad and I had to give up driving. I told Irene I'd saved $17,000 since there is no reason to buy the Olds. She asked why I didn't choose a more expensive car. That made sense, so now I've saved $43,000 by not buying a Lincoln Mark VIII. My brother-in-law suggested I consider a BMW and save even more. I told him I couldn't. I only buy American cars.

(149) Critters

Let me use the language of physics: Life without a dog is a half-life. Only God, a baby, and a dog can love you the way you think you deserve. You get adulation.

But babies grow up, and God often seems elsewhere. A dog is there everyday.

You can live without a cat, but why should you? A cat lets you do the adulation. My cat, Hodge, is perfect — beautiful, graceful, imperial, unhurried, a law unto himself. Isn't that what perfection is? I think God made cats to show what he could do when he really tried.

(150) Enjoying Bigotry

On my front lawn last Saturday, I found a bright-colored booklet titled "What's Behind the New World Order?" (Sub-title: "The Hidden Agenda Almost No One Dares to Discuss.") It came in a plastic sack and was distributed to every house in the neighborhood. It was a rich piece of anti-Catholic literature. I was glad to get it.

By comparison with pamphlets I read in my youth, the document was unimaginative. It said the Roman church is planning to take over the world and that the Pope is the Antichrist prophesied in Revelation. (You wanted to say, "Hey, we *knew* that!") The only fresh insight was that it was Rome which changed the Sabbath from Saturday to Sunday, and that change is the celebrated Mark of the Beast.

I'm Catholic, but none of his bothered me. Indeed, I was nostalgic. The pamphlet made me feel 12 years old growing up in Black River Falls, Wisconsin. I served Mass every day, and I was titillated by lurid booklets describing tortures of the Inquisition and orgies in the convents. Those were happy days.

So "What's Behind the New World Order?" had a good effect. I enjoyed it. And it won't do any harm.

It offers 80 pages of clumsy and unfocused writing. No one – not even a committed bigot – is going to read it.

(151) A Marital Challenge

After we were married seven years, Irene got the notion I wasn't very sentimental. I didn't pay attention to her and say nice things. I didn't, she charged, even know what color her eyes were. This was a nasty challenge.

Immediately I speculated. I knew my eyes were hazel, and baby Nick's eyes were bright blue. What color did Irene's eyes have to be? I couldn't figure it out. I'd learned about dominant and recessive genes in high-school biology. That was 20 years before, and I had forgotten it all. Finally, I resorted to a reasonable guess. I said, "Of course I know what color your eyes are. They're blue." I spoke with absolute confidence.

I must have been right. Irene became congenial again, and the question never recurred. If there's a moral here, I guess it's that you should pay attention in biology class.

(152) Doctors Discuss Old Age

Doctors have ways of making you feel old. When Irene had a pulled muscle in her shoulder, she complained that it still hurt, months after she injured it. Dr. deGruy said, "Mrs. McDonald, if you were 20, it would have cleared up in two weeks." (Thanks, Doc, she needed that.)

Yesterday I talked to Dr. Ball about having a cataract removed from my left eye. He said we can do it, and tried to schedule a time for the operation. He said, "We can do it this month or next month or next year. The matter isn't urgent. We can . . ." I cut him off. "Doc," I said, "I'm 67 years old. Trust me, it's urgent."

Dr. Rogers, my dentist, doesn't like to use the O-word. When he tells me some of my fillings are giving way, he says, "They're worn ... they're not .. Dan, you've had them a long time." I appreciate his delicacy.

I cheered his attitude last month when he put a ceramic filling in one of my teeth. He said, "It won't last as long as a silver filling, but ..." Then he paused. He didn't want to finish his sentence. I asked, "How long will the ceramic filling last?" He said, "It will be good for 20 years, I'm sure." "Don't sweat it, Doc," I told him. "The ceramic filling will do fine."

(153) Heeere's Dan-neee!

Every day I walk in the woods with Boswell, my golden retriever. In spring, we hear the sounds of baseball games played on the South Alabama campus. Mainly we hear the loudspeaker at Stanky Field and the energetic sports-announcer. Every Jaguar batter is introduced with enthusiasm. He says, "Heere's Willl-eee Dav-en-innng!" and "Heere's Looo-iss Hamm-ill-tahhhn!" After each introduction, the crowd roars encouragement.

I think this is wonderful. Willy Davening could be a second-string utility-infielder who hasn't had a hit all year. But with that introduction and crowd-noise, how could he fail to line one to right?

This is what we all need, but rarely get. I remember, on my wedding day, I was staying in a basement-room in Irene's mother's house. That morning when I started upstairs, I heard the family bustling around making preparations. I heard someone ask, "Who's that coming up?" Irene looked over the rail and said, "It's only Dan." (On my wedding day, I was "only Dan.") As I've thought about it through 40 years of marriage, it seems to me she could have cried out, "Hey, it's Dan-neee Mc-Donnn-ald!" And it wouldn't have hurt her family to come up with a brief cheer.

The marriage has turned out fine, so I guess I should be grateful. And I am. Still . . .

(154) Speak of the Devil

The *National Inquirer* reports that a terrified California family believes it is being stalked by the Devil. As one piece of evidence, they tell how their 17-year-old daughter was taking a shower when a black form entered her room and turned off the radio.

I'll bet it was the Scorpions singing "Rock Me Like a Hurricane."

(155) Watch Those Exclamation-Marks!!

Teaching the last day of our program on writing, I gave the Elderhostel class my usual counsel about punctuation. I told them to write with periods and commas. I said that six semi-colons and six exclamation-marks should last them the rest of their lives.

I referred scornfully to a document they'd received from the local Elderhostel office. It ended with the line "Have a Great Week!!" With dramatic intensity, I insisted that repetitive punctuation is as evil as repetitive language. I said one exclamation-mark is bad enough, and two in a row is an abomination.

After class, a lady sitting up front showed me the evaluation-form she had filled out for the program. It contained the line "Dr. McDonald is a wonderful,

wonderful teacher!!!" She asked, "Should I change this?"
"Leave that alone," I said. "It looks just fine."

(156) Getting the Picture

I'm just back from a 2-week Elderhostel trip in Italy.
I saw 50 incredible scenes — and 5,000 photographers.

Tourists stood before the greatest art and architecture of the western world, and ignored it. They faced Titian and Tinteretto paintings and looked at their light-meters. In Venice, they entered the splendor of St. Mark's; in Padua, they walked the holy stones of St. Anthony's — and their invariable response was "Can we take flash in here?" I saw one man looking across the lagoon to San Giorgio's, the incredible Palladian church. He said, "I don't need to go there; I have a telephoto lens."

Can't people distinguish between life and a photo-opportunity? I guess not. Irene says that when she taught at Julius T. Wright, a local girls' school, the students were anxious, and even desperate, to go to the proms — so they could have their pictures taken. Even if they didn't enjoy the dance or like their dates, the girls had to have those photos, so they could exchange them.

None of this is new. Over the years, I've seen tourists — not all of them Japanese — snapping like mad in the Prado and the Alamo, at Niagara Falls and Lake Inisfree, in Versailles and Westminster Abbey. These are places where nature and history and the human adventure have an overpowering effect, for some people. Last year I saw two men walking through Terragona, a 13th-century Spanish cloister. One said, "Are you using a Leica M6? I hear they're great."

#62 – "POOR DAN"

You wonder how these photographers respond to everyday life. You wonder how they spent their honeymoon. I have a vision of holy tourists arriving in Heaven and facing the Beatific Vision. I hear them asking, "Can we take flash up here?"

(157) "Price Varies"

You need to know how to order seafood when eating out at the Gulf. The good restaurants offer shrimp for $12.95 and scamp for $13.95. They also have freshly-caught fish. Here the menu says "Market Price" or "Price Varies."

Listen now. "Market Price" means they want your right arm and left leg. "Price Varies" means they can demand your next-born son. Don't get crazy. Order the scamp.

(158) No, Madonna, No

It's still an issue what I'm going to do in my retirement, but I know what I'm not going to do. I was much impressed by the London film-critic who panned *Body of Evidence*, then announced, "This newspaper has declared itself a Madonna-free zone." I can do that. I can make my retirement a Madonna-free zone.

Look at the trash and unpleasantness I can ignore. This morning's paper tells me Heidi Somebody, a California madam, is preparing to name celebrities who used her services. I don't need to know that. The tabloids churn out details (the charges and counter-charges) of the Burt Reynolds divorce, and the Roseanne Barr divorce, and the Michael Jackson divorce. None for me, thanks. Last week, cable TV gave me a choice between *Beverly Hills Cop 2* and *Kickboxer 3*. Tonight, network TV wants me to watch *My Mother Was an Alien*. Who needs this?   At movie-theaters this week, I can see *Surf Ninjas* or *Jason Goes to Hell* (another "Friday the 13th" blood-letting).   My radio blares teenage music, frenzied pizza commercials, and a DJ named Big Rodney.   The best-seller list offers me a new Danielle Steel romance and something called *Women Who Run With the Wolves*.

To all this, I say, "No. No, thank you. I live in a Madonna-free zone."

(159) Suspicious Minds Want to Know

City people up north aren't really hostile; they just seem that way.   Many are suspicious.   They're convinced you will cheat them if you get a chance.

I remember a wiry, 50-year-old woman who worked at a Shell station in New Jersey.   She gave me a tank of gas, and I gave her my Shell card.   When she brought the receipt, I signed it. She started to compare my signature with the one on the card and discovered I had never signed the back of my card. She was adamant, saying, "You have to sign this."   So I did.   Then she carefully compared the two signatures — the one I had just signed on the card and the one I had just signed on the receipt.   She looked at them for 30 seconds. Then she conceded.   "OK," she said, "I guess they match."

Pulling away, I wanted to ask her how far we were from Cape May.   But I didn't.   She'd just wonder what I meant by that.

(160) The Search for Meaning

At 5:00 last Saturday, I decided to enjoy an hour of male pleasure.   Irene was away someplace, and I had a chance to look at *Baywatch*. Some of my buddies had recommended it, and Jerry Seinfeld (on his show) admitted he always records the program. So I was ready. I poured out a bowl of Planters Peanuts, opened a bottle of Red Dog, switched on Channel 3, and settled back.

Baywatch began with pictures of sunrise over a California beach. Then I saw three seagulls circling around. Two young men sat at the lifeguard station talking about Father's Day. One told how his father died in a heroic rescue many years before. Then came a long flashback showing the fiery event. After that, I saw an aerial view of the beach filled with swimmers. Then, offshore, there was a boat on fire. The lifeguards swam out to help, the one wondering if he could be a hero like his father was. The boat was saved. Then came a commercial, and I opened another Red Dog.

When the program resumed, the camera panned in on two boys cavorting near the water, and one of them fell into something. I watched the other boy try to save him, fail, and then run down the beach screaming for help. Hearing his cries, the two lifeguards and some other young men jumped in a yellow Jeep and raced to aid the trapped boy. During the ride, the one lifeguard wondered if he could be a hero like his father. Finally they reach the place where the boy fell in. And . . .

That was it. I had had enough. *Baywatch* had gone on for 25 minutes, and I hadn't seen anything memorable, anything with redeeming significance. I felt cheated. I switched over to Channel 41 (Turner Classic Movies). They were showing a 1940s thriller, *I Wake Up Screaming*, which starred Betty Grable and Carol Landis. "Hey!" I thought. I walked into the kitchen and opened a Red Dog.

(161) The Rage to Live

Following months of dental-work, my sister-in-law Betty had to have a gall-bladder operation. In preliminary discussions, her surgeon listed possible dangers of the procedure, including death on the operating-table. Here, Betty protested. "I can't die, doctor," she said. "I've got all new teeth."

(162) The Mark of the TSAEB

Here's a tabloid story that will set you thinking. According to the *Weekly World News*, Richard Palmer, a New York-based biblical scholar, has established that the "Mark of the Beast" in Revelation is not 666. Translators looked at the figure upside-down. The number should be 999. Palmer didn't want to reveal this. He feared "Christianity could be shaken to its foundations."

I have a reason to welcome this news. Working from a simple numerical progression (A=6, B=12, C=18, etc.), the name "DANIEL MCDONALD" totals 666.

The story got me thinking about other scholarly errors. Is there a text somewhere that says "Wow!" when it should have said "Mom!"? I remember a character in Ira Levin's *The Stepford Wives* named "Dis" – was his name really "Sid"? Is our legal drinking-age derived from a statute in some Latin country where people could drink at 12? I notice that "SOIL" written upside-down becomes "7105." I recall the biblical parable where the unjust steward asks a debtor what he owes the master, and the man answers 100 jars of oil. The steward says, "Take thy bill and write 50." Should that have been "Take thy bill and write, "SO?"

It's probably a mistake to think about these things too much.

(163) Keeper of the Flame

Last month I heard a disturbing conversation. My wife and her sister were watching television and saw Emma Thompson glowing with youth and beauty. (Irene is now 62, and Betty is 69. Both are handsome, civilized women.) Irene asked, "Do you remember being young and pretty?" And Betty said, "No. You'll like this movie. It's about..." That was the answer — a quick "No."

Today when we talk of "the former Soviet Union," I wonder about other things. What happened to "the former Danny McDonald"? I have a photo of him leaping over a picnic-table in a Wisconsin park. What happened to "the former Molly McDonald," the joyous and exciting baby we adopted 30 years ago? What happened to "the former Patricia Severson" and "the former Ruth Sampson," the beauties who thrilled my youth (circa 1950)?

It doesn't help to describe these people today. (Danny is writing about his retirement. Molly and her husband run a dive-shop in St. Croix. Patricia and Ruth send me Christmas cards and talk about grandchildren.) *That's no answer!* Where are those "former" people?

You know, of course. They're in my head, and they enrich my life immeasurably. Walking in the woods with Boz, my golden retriever, I remember how it must have felt to jump a picnic-table. I think of shopping with 2-year-old Molly at Goldblatt's in South Bend. I'm back at Castle Hill drinking Blatz beer with Patricia and Ruth. (Maybe they don't remember being

young, pretty girls, but I sure do.) My "former"
people — dozens and dozens of them — are alive and
well.

I hope your memories are as rewarding.

(164) Buy Tomatoes from W.M.

Think about this one. An ad that appeared in *Parade*
and other magazines offers you a bush that grows
tomatoes 24 inches around. The offer comes from
W.M., a nationally-known authority whose many
commitments prevent him from giving his name.
Nevertheless, the words and promises you read are
genuinely his. To prove it, the ad includes a notary
public's signature and seal. These assure you you're
buying from the real W.M. and not from some impostor
pretending to be W.M.

If you think about this too long, you brain will
turn into wallpaper-paste.

(165) Hot as Hell

I worry about people who take Heaven and Hell
literally. They skirt all kinds of problems. I heard a
radio-preacher celebrating Paradise and the streets of
gold. He said, "There won't be any pot-holes in Heaven."
I wonder if he considered collateral issues: What will
we drive in Heaven? Where will we be going? Are
there speed limits?

I think of this because I'm looking at a 4-page
pamphlet published by the Fellowship Tract League of
Lebanon, Ohio. It's titled "The Burning Hell." The
cover shows a sinister devil-figure, a moustached villain
dressed in red. (He looks like Vincent Price playing
Cardinal Richelieu.) Above the title are the words:
"20,000 Degrees! And Not a Drop of Water!" They took

that drop-of-water reference from the Lazarus-Dives parable, but I can't imagine where they got the 20,000 degrees. They don't say if it's fahrenheit or centigrade.

Either way it is hotter than our sun, which burns at 10,000 degrees fahrenheit. We know this through spectroscopic analysis. As a scholar and a Christian, I have to wonder: Who spectroscoped Hell?

(166) A Tribute to Miss Thompson — 50 Years Later

Read over this Shakespearean song. There's a rich story (and a keen woman) related to it.

> Hark, hark! The lark at heaven's gate sings,
> And Phoebus 'gins arise,
> His steeds to water at those springs
> On chaliced flowers that lies,
> And winking Mary-buds begin
> To ope their golden eyes.
> With everything that pretty is,
> My lady sweet, arise!
> Arise, arise!

In 1942, when I was a freshman at Black River Falls High School, my English teacher made us memorize this poem. A dozen students (including me) had to stand up in class and recite it. And all of us had to write it on our semester exam.

This was no problem for me. I was good at memorizing poems, and lots of things in school didn't make much sense. Decades later, however, after I had a PhD and was a seasoned English professor, I began to wonder: Why did Miss Thompson make us learn *that*

#88 – "WHAT PRICE GENTILITY?"

poem? What could it mean to a 14-year-old growing up in rural Wisconsin?

I think I know the answer. Miss Thompson was enjoying an elaborate joke. I'm sure we were an unruly class (mostly boys). I imagine her getting fed up with our antics and saying, "I'll fix those little bastards! I'll make them memorize an obscure poem with strange words. I'll let them struggle with 'Phoebus' and "gins' and 'chaliced' and 'Mary-buds' and 'ope'." I'll watch them squirm waiting to recite it in class. That song will stick in their memory the rest of their lives."

Miss Thompson never explained anything. She didn't tell us the poem was addressed to grieving Imogen in *Cymbeline*. She didn't say it was about getting up on a bright spring morning. We had no idea who Phoebus was. We weren't sure that "ope" was short for "open." The word "'gins" was regularly pronounced *jins*.) But we didn't ask questions; we just memorized the poem. And, indeed, I have carried it in my head for 54 years.

I have no hard feelings toward Miss Thompson. Assigning "Hark, Hark! The Lark" was a brilliant practical joke, and I'm sure we deserved it. If I met her today (she'd be in her 70s), I'd shake her hand and buy her a drink and say, "Lady, you got me!"

(167) Ready, Aim, Fire, Shoot

Yesterday morning's paper told of Bobby Johnson, an Indianapolis loading-dock worker, who was arrested for firing six bullets into his 41-channel Zenith television. His complaint: There was nothing to watch. Charged with reckless behavior, Johnson said, "I don't see why a man can't shoot his own television if he wants to."

This didn't seem important to me until 11:30 last night when I couldn't sleep. I got up and began to surf the channels. (I can't read because of my glaucoma.) My choices included "Tales from the Crypt," "Messianic Judaism," "Evening at the Improv," the Psychic Television Network, an AMC movie starring Jerry Lewis, a demonstration of Power Walker Plus, a rerun of "The Partridge Family," a pitch for Victoria Principal cosmetics, a promo for *Golf Digest*, and a purring blonde who urged me to call 1-900-351-DOLL.

If I were arrested for shooting my television, I'd make late-night videotapes and play them in court. No jury would convict me.

(168) The Language of Contortion

In the gospel-reading last Sunday, Jesus said, "If anyone comes to me without turning his back on .his very self, he cannot be my follower." Driving home after Mass, I heard a radio-preacher complaining about modern infidelity. He said he was tired of "couples running around behind each other's backs."

I can't visualize these things.

(169) Weddings and Football

At St. Ignatius last month, a couple came up after 11:00 Mass to repeat their wedding-vows. They had been married 50 years. Standing by them were their daughters and grandchildren. With my usual sensitivity, I thought, "That poor bastard! Those freaking women conned him into this." As the ceremony went on (and on), I looked around the sanctuary. Women were touching their eyes with handkerchiefs. Men were checking their watches. It was almost time for the Miami-Jets game.

Then a large truth came to me: *Weddings are for women what football is for men*. There is a powerful emotional attraction, and neither group can explain it to the other.

(170) Mike Is 50

OK, it's time for a poem. I wrote this a few years ago to celebrate Mike Hanna's 50th birthday. It was read at his party.

> Mike is fifty — Shout hurray!
> His heart is fresh and green.
> He can do anything today
> He could at seventeen.

> This shows a life of honest toil,
> Of virtues pure and clean,
> Of principles aesthetic
> And an outlook bold and keen.

> It shows just how pathetic
> He was at seventeen.

You can only write this kind of poem about a dear friend.

(171) Airport Announcements

Killing time in the Atlanta airport last month, Irene and I were impressed by the loudspeaker announcements. We heard, "Sally Hendricks. Sally Hendricks. Please see your nearest Delta representative." We wondered what Sally was going to hear. Then it occurred to us we might have messages broadcast. And we had fun coming up with these announcements:

"Jay Gatsby. Jay Gatsby. Meet your party in the central lobby."

"Graham Greene. Graham Greene. See your nearest Continental Agent."

"Manon Lescaut. Manon Lescaut. Please check with Immigration."

"Emily Post. Emily Post. Please pick up a white telephone. You have a courtesy call."

"Hester Prynne. Hester Prynne. Go to the Security Office on Concourse A." [and]

"Moll Flanders. Moll Flanders. Report to Baggage Pickup."

We should have had some of these broadcast throughout the terminal. Nobody would mind. Most people would miss the allusions. And those who recognized them would enjoy a chuckle.

The problem is once you start this game, it's hard to quit. Even now, I find myself walking down the hall thinking: "Alice Liddell. Please report to Lost and Found." "Gregor Samsa. Please . . ."

(172) Of Race, Prose, Sex, and Simplicity

At Barnes & Noble this afternoon, I saw a display of books set up for Black History Month. Prominent among them was one titled *Satisfying Black Men Sexually*. This, I had to look at.

Opening the cover, I saw it was by a Dr. Rosie Milligan, and the full title was *Satisfying Black*

Men sexually – Made Simple. The book had 185 pages.

My first thought was that a book called *Satisfying Dan McDonald Sexually – Made Complex* would take one page. With a bad writer, maybe a page and a half. I guess this says something about black men, prose, simplicity, and me. I don't want to think about it.

(173) "This Will Appear in *Sagacity*"

Yesterday I paged through *Writer's Market*, then mailed off articles to *Michigan Quarterly*, *Sewanee Review*, and *Sagacity*. I especially hope that last one is accepted. When I read the essay, I want to say, "Yes, this will appear in *Sagacity* next month."

I could do worse. Literary magazines have strange titles. I don't want to tell people, "That article was published in *Bad Haircut*." Or "Last year, I had an essay in *Boing-Boing* and a poem in *Hobo Jungle*." Happily, my stuff wouldn't fit in *Pig Iron*. They want "works that address alienation, the unconscious, loss, despair, and historical discontinuity." (It must be fun having a drink with the editors.)

Regrettably, I have no essays for the erotic journals. It would be interesting to send them something, even if it's rejected. I could report, "I was turned down by *Buxom*; I couldn't get into *Yellow Silk*; and I never achieved *Climax*."

You get crazy if you start worrying about the titles on your bibliography. I've had articles in *Negative Capability* and *et cetera*. Neither sounds impressive, but they're first-rate journals. I've had poems in *Theology Today* and *Sexology Today*. After that, I thought I was a shoo-in for *Psychology Today*, but *Psychology Today* went out of business.

So what's left? I'm going to send articles to the literary journal at Northwestern University. Then I can announce, "This next essay has been accepted for publication by *Triquarterly*. I don't know when they're going to print it."

(174) The First Time Around

Is the song right? Is love lovelier the second time around? Maybe, but it's also nice the first time around once you're old enough to be doing it the second time around. It's wonderful when you're old enough so marriage craziness doesn't get to you. I am now 68, and I want to go on record that I am *almost* there.

(175) Ask "Personality Parade"

On the second page of *Parade*, we see "Personality Parade," a column which answers questions from readers. The headline says, "Want the facts? Opinion? Truth? Write Walter Scott." I suppose this provides a service, but I worry about some of the correspondents.

Were there really people sitting around the house wondering:

- How tall is Snoop Doggy Dogg?

- Why doesn't Peter Sampras' family attend his tennis matches?

- Did Danielle Steel have trouble getting her first novel published?

- Whatever became of Ramiro Martinez, the Texas police-officer who shot berserk sniper Charles Whitman in 1966?

• Does Marla Maples have brothers and sisters?

I have questions for Walter Scott: Who are the people who send you letters? Are they for real? What do they do all day?

(176) The Coward's Way

A recent news-story quotes action star Jean-Claude Van Damme as boasting, "I've divorced three gals but they're still my friends." What's the big deal? Anyone can be friends with a woman if he's not married to her. That's the coward's way.

(177) "Stewardess"

On a recent flight from Puerto Rico, I wanted to get a second beer and called out "Stewardess." Irene corrected me, insisting I should have said "Flight Attendant." I was politically incorrect by calling attention to the girl's gender. Usually I support political correctness. (I don't say "nigger" or "fag," and I don't like people who do.) But this is crazier than I want to get.

Why can't I call attention to the girl's gender? She's been working for 15 years to call attention to her gender. As a teenager, she watched her diet; she played with jewelry, color, fashion, hairstyle, and makeup, trying to be a pretty girl. Delta Airlines hired her because she *was* a pretty girl. She spent the morning of the day I saw her fixing her hair and makeup and jewelry and uniform (blue skirt, white blouse, fancy red scarf) to make herself an especially pretty girl. After all this, am I supposed to call out "Hey, ungendered unit, I'd like another Budweiser"?

#31 - "DADDY AND REX"

I'm older now, and I probably don't understand current issues. Still, I can't see anything wrong with a flight-attendant's being a pretty girl and with my saying "Steward*ess*." Is being a woman some kind of guilty secret (like incest or leprosy)? Is it a shameful circumstance nobody should mention?

(178) Old-Time Coffee

For the three years since it opened, Delchamps Supermarket in the Spring Hill Shopping Center has offered free coffee. When you entered the store, there on your immediate right was a table with two large coffee-pots (one regular and one decaffeinated). And as long as I can remember, both pots were empty. There was never any coffee. Sometimes I'd tell a cashier they should build a new pot, but nothing ever happened.

Now things have changed. The management has taken away the table and the coffee-pots. They're not offering coffee at all. I want to write in to complain about this, but I'm not sure how to define the problem.

(179) An Act of God

After Hurricane Erin struck the Gulf Coast, the "Sound Off" column in the *Mobile Press* spoke regularly of divine purpose. One caller insisted Mobile wasn't "lucky" (as an editorial had claimed): "It was blessed." Another knew God sent Erin to warn Alabamians not to legalize gambling.

This produced interesting responses. One caller observed that the storm had ruined the pecan-crop in Baldwin County. Was God telling us not to eat pecans? Another noted that Erin had swerved away from the casinos in Biloxi. Why were they blessed if gambling is so bad? One wag suggested the storm was a warning to people who left the toilet-seat up.

I'm impressed by the notion of a god who looks down and says, "We hit Florida hard last year. I'll aim the storm over toward Alabama. It will by-pass Mobile; the city has 200 churches. But I know there's a lot of sin in Robertsdale, so..." This is a god with too much time on his hands.

The ultimate claim of God's overseeing providence came on the *Miracle Revival Hour* last month. Radio preacher David Paul said, "It's no accident you're listening to this broadcast. The fact you are hearing this sermon was ordained by God before the creation of the earth." Wow! Talk about micromanagement!

(180) "Hit It Big at the Belle"

Colorful TV ads are urging Mobilians to drive to Mississippi and gamble at the Biloxi Belle. Kenny Stabler and others are telling us to "Hit it big at the Belle." Indeed, this is my retirement goal.

I'm savvy enough to know what "hit it big" means. It never means "Win some money and take it home." It means "Win some money (maybe) and have a good time losing it before you go." On Saturday I met a lady who said that on her first pull at the slot machine, she won $460. I asked how much she came home with, and she said she lost it all. My son Nick sat with a friend who was $370 up at the blackjack table. Nick gave him good counsel ("Richie, get your ass out of Dodge"), but of course Richie didn't listen. He stayed, lost the $370, and lost the $200 stake he came in with.

Isn't all this like my retirement? I'm not going to walk away from it a big winner. But I can have fun and play a long time. I can't complain about the odds at the Biloxi Belle. (At the dice-table, if I make 8 the hard way — that's a 1-in-36 chance — they pay me 9 to 1.) I get worse odds at Dr. Broughton's office. He told me if I live to be 80, my chance of having severe prostate trouble is 100 percent. When I was in the clinic being treated for high blood-pressure, I saw a sign on the wall. It announced "The Four Major Causes of Hypertension." The first two were being male and being 40 years old. To quote Brett Maverick's daddy, "What kind of odds is that?"

I see my retirement as a lush casino. I plan to enjoy the game and hang around for years. I expect to hit it big at the Belle.

(181) Cruel and Inhuman Punishment

The Association of Attorneys General just released its "Top 10" list of frivolous lawsuits filed by prisoners. My favorite is *Jackson v. Barton*. Here, a convict sued because lightning had knocked out the prison TV satellite-dish, and he was forced to watch network shows.

Now we'll see new books on the history of torture. They'll show prisoners enduring the rack, the branding-iron, the thumb-screw, the iron-maiden, and reruns of *Roseanne*.

(182) Jumping to Conclusions

In *The Language of Argument*, I warned people not to jump to conclusions. It's unreasonable to say, "Running is dangerous: look what happened to Jim Fixx." Or "All labor-leaders are crooks — just like Jimmy Hoffa." I called this "Induction with an Insufficient Sample" and declared it was bad argument.

Today I'm not so sure. I look around me and see dozens of places where I make instant judgments:

- I turned on WHIL this morning and heard a Liszt concerto. It sounded like someone attacking a piano with a snow-shovel, so I turned it off. I had listened for five seconds.

- In Scotland last year, they served me haggis. (It's a dish made with parts of the sheep nobody mentions.) I took one bite and announced I hated it.

- Last week, a voice on the phone began, "Congratulations! You've just won a free trip to Disney World and . . ." I interrupted, "Thanks for calling. But I'm not interested." (I say the same thing when I hear, "Hi, my name is Debbie. How are you today?")   "

- At Mass last Sunday, Father Rogers began his sermon dramatically. He intoned, "Faith," and paused for 10 seconds. Then he repeated "Faith" and paused again. I don't know what he said after that. I tuned him out.

- At a party at the Hannas', I picked up a beer in the kitchen, then strolled around the patio looking for an interesting conversation to join. In one group, I saw a man lecturing at three women. I heard, "young people today . . ." I walked on to find another conversation.

- Last summer, I read William F. Buckley's column in the morning paper. In the second sentence, he used the phrase "biblical irridentism." I don't know what he said in the third sentence.

- Jud and I went to have lunch at Hooters last week. In the parking-lot, when we were 20 feet from the door, we could hear rock music blaring inside. I said, "Let's eat at Barnes & Noble."

Despite these examples, my textbook isn't wrong. People shouldn't form hasty opinions. If I'd listened to that sermon on Faith, it might have been profound. If I'd read further in the Bill Buckley column, I might have learned something. To make rational judgments, we need to see a body of evidence.

Indeed, when Jud and I were about to leave the Hooters parking-lot, we met one of the waitresses coming to work. A trim blonde, she wore orange shorts, a cut-off T-shirt, and a name-tag that said "Bambi." She smiled, "How are you boys today?" — and we watched her walk into the restaurant. Jud asked, "Does that music really bother you?" "Let's go in," I said. "I'll get used to it."

As the book says, "To make rational judgments, we need to see a body of evidence."

(183) "Draft" Is a Difficult Concept

Cherie Graves told me a rich story about waitressing at the Oyster House in Gulf Shores. A middle-aged man ordered a bottle of Miller Genuine Draft. She told him, "We don't have that in bottles, but we have it on tap." "I don't want that," he said. "Bring me a Budweiser."

(184) Dream Women

I fell in love with Kiri Te Kanawa seven years ago when she sang Rosalinde in a televised production of *Die Fledermaus*. She was gorgeous and vivacious, and she sang like an angel. I told my wife, "I'm sorry, honey. I'm in love with another women." Irene didn't mind. She thought Kiri was pretty special too.

Then last year, things got complicated. I went to Barnes & Noble to arrange a reading of my essays and I met the manager, Nancy Anlage. She was beautiful and charming and intelligent, and I just knew she sang like an angel. When we left the store, I told Irene, "Nancy is incredible. I may be unfaithful to Kiri Te Kanawa." Irene didn't mind. She thought Nancy was incredible too. She asked, "Couldn't you have two dream-women?" I said I'd try.

This worked fine until last Saturday when we heard the Metropolitan Opera production of Gounod's *Faust*. The soprano who sang Marguerite was overwhelming. What a voice! Afterward, I asked Irene who she was. She said, "That's Renee Fleming." Then she held out a copy of *Opera News* and said, "Here's a picture of her." *Wham!* It happened again.

Now things were getting out of hand. Should I be untrue to Kiri Te Kanawa and Nancy Anlage? Was that the act of a gentleman? Again, Irene's sanity saved the day. She said, "You're 69, Dan. Perhaps three dream-women would be too much for you." She was right, of course. So, despite Renee Fleming's wonderful qualities, I am going to remain faithful to Kiri Te Kanawa and Nancy Anlage. Sure, I'll suffer for a while, but I'll get over it. A man has to honor his commitments.

However, as a gentleman, I plan to send a telegram explaining things to Renee Fleming. It will clarify the difficult situation and conclude, "I'm sorry, Renee. But you know how it is."

(185) A Complex Masquerade

A few years ago, radio evangelist John R. Douglas made a serious accusation. He charged, "The National Council of Churches is masquerading as a wolf in sheep's clothing." If you can figure that out, you're smarter than I am.

(186) Let's Hear It for the *News*

I may be America's most dedicated reader of the *Weekly World News.* It's obvious when you talk to me. I know about a lot of stuff.

I don't just glance at the tabloid headlines ("Sunbathing Man Bursts into Flames!" or "Dutch Ventriloquist Speaks from Beyond the Grave"). I read the stories; I read them all the way through. Give me a test. Ask me about the Brazilian native who has his head on backwards. Ask who is the reincarnated Joan of Arc, or how to identify a space-alien, or where the Holy Grail has just been located, or the exact date of Judgment Day. I know. I'm *au courant.*

I rejoice in the regular columns. Leskie Pinson's "Around the World" has provocative stories. My favorite concerns a Bombay native who was arrested for walking through the streets naked. He said he thought he was invisible. Ed Anger's "My America" is a continuing delight. But I doubt he'll ever surpass his major efforts: "Pave the Stupid Rain Forest," "Ban Anti-Smoking Wimps," and "Let's Build the Nixon Memorial."

I love the psychic columnists. As a betting man, I was pleased when Countess Sophia announced who'll win the Super Bowl in 2008. (Answer: the Moscow Bears.) As a scholar, I was thrilled when Serena counseled a man who thought he was Leonardo da Vinci. I have days like that.

I read the ads. In "The Billboard," Karen Hart says she can bring back my lost love. A lending agency will bring back my lost income ("VISA/

#70 - "BROTHERS"

Mastercard: Bad credit, no credit, no problem"). Whisper XL promises I can eavesdrop on conversations 100 feet away. And Ekses in San Bernardino offers me "One Free Incantation. No Charge." Where else can I find these things?

I relish the Page 5 Girl and the other beauties who display themselves throughout the pages. Some days, however, I look at the pictures, and I suspect they're all the same girl. I hope the paper pays her a lot.

I never miss the Giant Horoscope. Serena Sabak may be "Astrologer to the Rich and Famous," but she always has kind words for a Leo. She just told me to prepare for an adventure because "your energy and will-power will peak on Monday."

I was distressed last year when the *Weekly World News* printed an "Elvis Dies" story. But this week's headline suggests that Elvis — like Hitler and JFK — may still be alive. I have new hope.

I await the next issue.

(187) The Truth about Adoption

I just met Sam Rogers, and we immediately became good friends. That's because we're both teachers, and we both adopted babies.

Adoptive parents have joyous experience in common, and they need to talk about it. (Even if it happened 30 years ago.) Sam and I were like football-fans who discover they were both at the Saints game when Tom Dempsey kicked that 63-yard field-goal. We're brothers.

I told Sam a story bout my years with adopted Molly. When she was four and we now had Nicholas and Rebecca (both homemade), a lady in South Bend asked me a direct question. She said, "Can you really love your adopted child as you do your natural-born children?" I told her the truth. "Oh, no," I said, "you can never love your other children the way you love your first child."

(188) Literate People Are More Fun

It's nice to have a cultured wife. Last Sunday after Mass, Irene and I went grocery-shopping at Delchamps. We got separated for a while; then I found her standing in front of the beverage shelf. She was surveying bottles of Perrier, Ice Mountain, Polish Spring, Quest, and Clearly Canadian. I asked what she was looking for. Instantly, she said, "I came to Casablanca for the waters."

(189) Rachael's Psychic Experience

My friend Rachael Richardson stopped by my office last week and surprised me with her news. Rachael is retired from the University where she worked for a long time with the Graduate School. I've always thought of her as super-keen and super-businesslike. Now she tells me she is writing a book about psychic experience.

Rachael *believes*. She thinks psychics can tell us secret truths. She said, "Whenever I hear the phone ring, I know who it is." She said, "Sometimes I get a feeling about an old friend and I call them up. Invariably, I reach them on a crucial day." She said, "It's foolish to pay $5 a minute to a telephone-psychic. A good local psychic will charge $25 an hour." I sat there and listened to that.

I see the psychic landscape — the mystic world of ESP, PK, astrology, psychometry, etc. — as nut country.

(Except for the con-artists who prosper there.) Still, Rachael isn't weird. She's a bright and articulate lady. I told my wife at supper, "Rachael may be right, and I may be wrong – but I don't think so." I thought about this late into the night. I concluded, "Maybe we all believe what we need to believe."

(190) Jumping Jehovah!

When I talk about God, I imagine a force that works for good, a force I don't understand. There may be better ways to think about divinity, but there are also worse ways.

It's easy see God as a plantation-owner who lives up in the big house. After all, our prayers and hymns are anthropomorphic. They show God trampling out the vineyard, keeping his eye on the sparrow, and holding the faithful in the palm of his hand. Still, when you confine divinity, when you reduce it to human terms, you get weird images.

Last week I heard a preacher on *The Living Word* assure us "God is faster than a speeding bullet and able to leap tall buildings at a single bound." I imagined Him stretching in front of the World Trade Center and thinking, "I hope I clear both towers."

Yesterday on WMOB, I heard an evangelist yearn for the afterlife when he will know God better. He said, "Now we see through a glass darkly, but then it will be eyeball to eyeball."

I think of these things because this morning on *Love Worth Finding*, Dr. Adrian Rogers insisted God is still in charge of things and there is no panic in Heaven. He said, "The Holy Trinity never meets in emergency session."

A meeting of the Trinity? I can't help imagining
the inter-office memo:

```
                    DATE: Now

FROM: The Father

TO: The Son

COPY: The Holy Spirit

We need a meeting to talk about
Asia, the moons of Jupiter, and Sally
Johnson who wants to move back to
Cleveland.

These are urgent issues. I have
reserved the Executive Board Room
for yesterday at 2:00 p.m. Please
be on time.
```

Yes, this is strange. But it's what happens when you
make God human. You end up like the San Francisco
seamstress whose heart stopped on the operating-table.
Her story appeared in the *Weekly World News*, headlined: "I Saw God and He Looks Like Charlton Heston."
    I prefer the language of *Star Wars*: "May the
Force be with you."

(191) The News

The story took a full page in the *Weekly World News*.
It announced an important discovery, one that "put
history buffs on cloud nine." It was celebrated as "the
sensational find of the decade."
    What was discovered? It was a studio photograph
of a family. Carl Chafin, a historian, found the picture

in the musty files of the *San Francisco Examiner* and identified the six people on it. Chafin was thrilled. He announced, "This is the only picture anyone has ever seen of Wyatt Earp as a teenager."

I guess that's what they call a slow-news day.

(192) The Bacchus Room

Last month, Irene and I toured the elegant Villa Pisano outside Venice. I was impressed by one special room. On the walls were paintings of classical gods. Female figures were dancing; men were drinking and eating grapes. This was a place for parties. It was called the Bacchus Room.

As of yesterday, I have renamed my den. I don't host many parties there, and I have no paintings of gods or dancing girls. But it's where I drink a couple of beers before supper. I will think of it as my "Bacchus Room" every time I pop a can of Red Dog.

(193) Explaining Death

When my son was 10, he twice asked me about death. With the courage that has made me a legend, I avoided the question.

The first time, I recalled *Rosencrantz and Guildenstern are Dead* and said "Death is not being on a boat sailing to England." Apparently that wasn't evasive enough because a week later, Nick came back and asked again. This time I resorted to biology. I told him, "Death is a condition when your nucleoproteins are no longer capable of autoreproduction." That did it. He didn't ask again.

I did a better job in my Modern Drama class. One morning, we finished Synge's *Riders to the Sea*, and we were shaken by its depiction of death and the inevitability of dying. I told students I knew a good way to handle the issue. I said, "Go eat at the Cafeteria this noon, and on your way through the line, pick up a piece of lemon pie. Then when you're done with the regular meal, wash out your mouth with water. Now take a big forkful of that pie and hold it on your tongue. Think to yourself, 'I'm going to die someday, but screw that! This is great lemon pie'."

If you know a better way to talk of death, I'm happy for you.

(194) Man, That Hurts!

Look over this piece of deconstructionist prose. I don't ask you to read it because nobody can read it. Just glance at it, and see what you think.

> We would not, however, assert that this nonsemiotic meaning of the word *communication*, as it works in ordinary language, in one or more of the so-called natural languages, constitutes the *literal* or *primary* [*primitif*] meaning and that consequently the semantic, semiotic, or linguistic meaning corresponds to a derivation, extension, or reduction, a metaphoric displacement. We would not assert, as one might be tempted to do, that semio-linguistic communication acquired its title *more metaphorico*, by analogy with "physical" or "real" communication, inasmuch as it also serves as a passage, transporting and transmitting something, rendering it accessible.

That's from Jacques Derrida's *Signature Context*. It says, in effect, that words don't mean much, that one piece of literature is as good as another, and that (Let's hear it for political correctness!) Dickens' mother probably wrote better than he did.

Why do I burden you with this? Well, a few weeks ago, I gave a reading from my manuscript-essays at Barnes & Noble. I sent invitations to a few people. And my friend Tim Lally wrote to say he couldn't make it. He had to drive up to Tuscaloosa to hear a talk by Jacques Derrida.

He sure knows how to hurt a guy.

(195) 49ers ±38 - Cowboys ±28

In the NFC Championship game last Sunday, San Francisco led Dallas 31-14 at halftime. But sports-commentator Terry Bradshaw gave us the true picture. He said, "If you don't count those first three scores (which came on turnovers), Dallas is leading 14-10." Boy, that made me think.

If you don't count things . . . If you don't count my age, gender, and birthplace, I'm somebody else. I could be your grandmother − or *you*. I could be an historical figure, though history wouldn't benefit much. I know me. I'd be Judas asking "Could you make that 30 pieces of gold?" I'd be Patrick Henry saying, "Let me rephrase that." I'd be Florence Nightingale complaining "I'm on my break." You get the idea.

Anyway when the championship game ended, the scoreboard read "San Francisco 38, Dallas 28." I didn't hear Terry Bradshaw on the post-game show, so I may never know what the real score was.

(196) Shopping Healthy

Irene is taking a LifeCare 55 course at the University,

If you had
finished
reading this
sentence,

and learning about diet and health. I may never
eat again.

Let me tell you about our visit to the
supermarket this morning.

Irene moaned happily wheeling through the
vegetable department. Pointing to items in her basket,
she exclaimed, "Isn't this wonderful!" Looking in, I
saw parsnips, broccoli, chard, turnips, romaine lettuce,
brussels sprouts, endive, and tofu. I muttered,
"Yummy."

At the candy display, I wanted to buy some
Brach caramels, but Irene warned against it. She said
excessive sugar impairs the body's use of Vitamin B. I
bypassed the caramels.

At the meat-counter, I was fool enough to suggest
hot-dogs for lunch. Irene said, "You had hot-dogs in
April." She meant I'd had Hormel 97% fat-free franks
two months ago. A man shouldn't get caught up in
springtime indulgence.

In the cereal aisle, Irene never mentioned sodium
content. I said, "How about some Grape Nuts? I like
Grape Nuts." She said, "No, you don't." Our shopping-
basket never slowed down.

In the next aisle, I bought some Hill & Brooks
regular coffee. (Irene prefers to brew decaffeinated,
two cups at a time.) She reminded me that caffeine
limits the body's absorption of calcium. She let
me buy my brand, but warned I had been drinking
too much coffee lately. "I haven't been counting,"
she said. "But it seems to me you're downing 5.62
cups a day." She made it sound like Russian
roulette.

At the dairy counter, Irene bought Lactate 10, a
product guaranteed to have no dairy-fat, and some

slimy yogurt. "I know you hate this," she said, "but you haven't tried it lately."

When I picked up some Kraft cheese (New York cheddar, extra sharp), she stared in horror. You'd think I was holding a live grenade. She said to put it back; she'd bought a healthier cheese for me. She held up a tiny bar of mozzarella, assuring me, "This is low salt, low fat, low everything." She added, "It tastes like soap, but we'll get used to it."

When we reached the bakery, it was time to salvage my manhood. (After all, I'd sold out not buying caramels or hot-dogs or Grape Nuts or cheddar cheese.) I picked up a sack of hard-rolls. Now Irene became philosophical. She said, "Dan, you're a free moral agent. Do what you want. If you want to gulp down empty calories and take years from your life and suffer as an invalid and die leaving me an inconsolable widow, you go ahead. You make the choice." Standing tall, I threw the sack in our basket. "Damn the torpedoes," I said.

Driving home from Delchamps, Irene didn't mention the hard-rolls. Instead, she was brave. She said we should try to enjoy the few years we have left. She promised to stay with me to the end.

(197) The Good Old Days

It's nice to be retired when so many American businesses are getting rid of workers. But they're doing it gently. They don't have lay-offs any more. Companies now speak of "down-sizing," "right-sizing," "furloughing," "indefinite idling," "accelerated retirement," and (a wonderful word) "derecruitment." It was cleaner in my day. We got fired.

But, even in my day, I could have used this
language. I didn't get married until I was nearly
thirty. So I spent years cruising in bars, and going
to parties, dances, and school-functions looking for
women who would respond to my charm. There
weren't many. But I don't remember those as years
of frustration — years of "No, Dan" and "I'm sorry, Dan"
and "Not tonight, Dan, I have to wash my hair."
Instead, I look back on them with an air of
triumph. I can celebrate them as my days of
derecruitment.

(198) Remembrance of Things Past

You can forget a lot in 50 years, and there's a lot you
can't forget.

At the reunion of the Black River Falls High
School, Class of '45, I kept discovering myself in other
people's memories. Gene Strasberg asked, "Do you
remember that huge box of comic-books you kept
under Calvin Clark's gas-stove?" Donn Waldum said I
always came to his house and played the piano. Jack
Kasik recalled the 14-mile hike we made with Boy
Scout Troop 59. Bruce Behlow spoke of a humor
column he and I wrote for the high-school paper.
Edgar Preston said we always met at the barber-shop.
I don't remember any of this. It's weird knowing I
have a secret life that exists in other people's heads.

But some things I can't forget. Lunch with
Patricia and Gene Elliott was pleasant and disturbing.
Irene and Gene spoke about problems of retirement.
Patricia and I discussed mutual friends and the
flourishing condition of our Wisconsin hometown. But I
wanted to talk about other things.

Patricia was my young love (1949 - 1953), and God! it was intense. She made me gloriously happy; she made me miserable. As she chatted about her family, I remembered walking back and forth in front of my phone working up courage to call her. I thought of the long letters I sent her and answers that sometimes never came. I wondered what she'd do if I cried out my teenage emotions.

I wanted to say, "Why didn't you return my phone-call to Minneapolis?" "Do you still have that bronze-color bathing-suit?" "Do you remember *Blue Tango?*" "Why did you run around with Jerry Tollesrud?" "Weren't those wonderful evenings drinking Blatz beer at Castle Hill?" "I still wear the silver cuff-links you gave me for Christmas." "Do you remember my '53 Chevy?" "Why didn't you come home that Easter weekend?" "Couldn't you at least have . . . " The lines raced through my head as I looked at this handsome, civilized lady in her early 60s. Patricia broke in, "Dannie, would you pass the salt please?" Handing it over, I said, "And how often do you see your grandchildren?"

Memories, memories. Irene summed up the class-reunion weekend. She said, "Nostalgia is hard work."

(199) Another Question for "Ask Marilyn"

Today's *Parade* prints a letter to Marilyn Vos Savant from Roberta Lee of Marquette Heights, Illinois. She has an emotional problem:

> Please help me. My co-workers think I'm crazy, and I don't know where else to turn for an answer. I say that limes are dyed green so that

they are more easily distinguished from lemons in the supermarkets. What's the truth?

Marilyn's answer is narrowly focused. She says it is lemons that are dyed (and treated) to make them more yellow.

She doesn't ask about Roberta, and her co-workers, and their place of employment. Why this frustration, why the frenzy worrying about lemons and limes? I'd have advised Roberta to quit her job at the battery plant. She's been breathing lead too long.

(200) Way to Go!

At my age, I have to think some about death — not abstract, philosophical death (Forget that!), but my own death. I believe I've got it figured out.

What I want least is probably what I'll get. I'll die in USA Medical Center with my family around me. I'll weigh 85 pounds and be full of tubes. My mind and spirit will have departed a month earlier. Who needs this?

There are better ways. If an airliner has to crash someplace, I'd just as soon go that way. I'd like to be traveling first-class on Delta. I'll be wearing my blue suit. I'll be drinking a Chivas-and-water and looking over the stewardess. We'll get the panic-news three minutes before the crash. (I hope someone survives to record my last words: "Come to think of it, I *will* have another scotch.") All this is my second favorite fantasy.

In my ultimate fantasy, I will be shot through the head by Mike Hanna. He's a dear friend, but he will be temporarily maddened by finding me in bed with his wife. The case will never come to trial. The

#200 – "WAY TO GO!"

District Attorney's Office will issue a statement saying: "The investigators and prosecutors agree there was no criminal action here. We have examined Dr. McDonald's character, Michael Hanna's emotional stability, and Nancy Hanna's style and beauty — and the event was an unfortunate but inevitable accident. No grand jury would bring in an indictment. We consider the case closed." In private conversations, the District Attorney will add: "The son-of-a-bitch had it coming."

If you don't like my death-fantasy, work out one of your own.

(201) Self-Publishing

Any way I write it, this is going to sound like sour grapes — but what the hell!

Why did I pay money to have this book printed? That's easy. Because no agent or publisher would touch it. I didn't have what it takes.

Lord knows I tried. I sent my manuscript to four publishers. Two said they liked it, and all four sent it back. I mailed it to three agents. Two said they loved it, and all three sent it back. They had good reason.

Publishers want books that will sell hundreds of thousands of copies. They achieve this in two ways. They print works by famous people. And they publish glitzy, titillating trash.

Look at the current *New York Times* list of best-selling non-fiction. It offers titles by Katherine Graham, Joseph Cardinal Bernardin, Jimmy Carter, Robert Coles, Walter Cronkite, Tanya Tucker, and Mia Farrow. These may be fine books, but I wonder if they'd have been printed if the authors were unknown. (I remember the

New York agent who phoned me and said, "If your name was Andy Rooney, I'd sign you right up.")

There are exceptions, of course. Some first-rate books appear on the best-seller list, and occasionally one by a newcomer. (Right now, *Angela's Ashes* is a big hit.) But this doesn't happen often.

Is it just petulant envy when I say most of the non-fiction is Hollywood trash? Well, look at the list. It includes *Murder in Brentwood*, *His Name Is Ron*, *Evidence Dismissed*, and *Outrage*. These lovingly scrutinize the O. J. Simpson murders. Other titles offer pop religion (*Conversations with God*), fantasy sociology (*The Millionaire Next Door*), glib psychology (*Men Are From Mars, Women Are From Venus*), teenage morality (*The Seven Spiritual Laws of Success*), and don't-you-wish medicine (*Dr. Atkins' New Diet Revolution* and *The Arthritis Cure*). Most of the titles have a sexy, titillating edge. There's *Midnight in the Garden of Good and Evil* (about a "strange death" in Savannah), *Reviving Ophelia* (on "dangers for teen-age girls"), *Journey Into Darkness* (on "vicious serial criminals"), and *The Kiss* (about a woman's "obsessive love-affair with her father").

I'm not making this up, friend. This is what's in the *Times*.

The list of paperback best-sellers offers more of the same. It has *Hitler's Willing Executioners* (enjoy another look at the Holocaust), *Care of the Soul* (get yourself a moral tuneup), *Sleepers* (see reformatory boys take revenge), *In Contempt* (more on the O. J. Simpson slashings), and *Mindhunter* (everything you ever wanted to know about serial killers). Also, there's *Private Parts* and *Bad As I Wanna Be* — insights from those eminent social critics, Howard Stern and Dennis Rodman.

By best-seller standards, my book didn't measure up. There's no obscenity. It's not about UFOs or suicide-cults or bisexuality or Madonna or poltergeists or torture or rape or New Age dieting. It talks about God a few times, but (except here) it never mentions O. J. Simpson. So I had to publish the book myself.

That's OK. I'm convinced there's an audience who will enjoy it.

INDEX OF TITLES

ORDER FORM

For copies of this book, write:

Daniel McDonald
2001 Old Bay Front Drive
Mobile, AL 36615

Enclose $12 for the first copy, and $10 for each additional copy. (This includes postage and handling.)

Please print or type (or write real neat).

NAME _____

ADDRESS_____

_____

CITY _____

STATE/ZIP_____

Allow six weeks for delivery, though you'll probably have it in three.